Spirituality in Counseling and Psychotherapy

The FACE-SPIRIT Model

Radha J. Horton-Parker
Old Dominion University

R. Charles Fawcett
University of Virgina

Dedications

To our greatest spiritual teachers ...

my father, Payne,

and my husband, Skip

—Radha

my father, Richard,

and my spiritual counselor, Glenda

—Charlie

Published by Love Publishing Company
P.O. Box 22353
Denver, Colorado 80222
www.lovepublishing.com

Library of Congress Catalog Card Number 2008927448

Copyright © 2010 by Love Publishing Company
Printed in the United States of America
ISBN 978-0-89108-341-2

Contents

Preface

Faith is an act of a finite being who is grasped by, and turned to, the infinite.

Paul Tillich

One of the most significant developments in the last quarter century has been the recognition of the importance of religion and spirituality in counseling and the helping professions. The literature on this subject is vast and growing. However, there is relatively little information dealing directly with the integration of spirituality into counseling and social work practice. In our research, we sought in vain for specific strategies suggesting holistic and pedagogically sound methodologies by which practitioners might integrate religion and spirituality into professional helping.

This book is an attempt to offer such a model. Our purpose in writing has been to develop a variety of concrete integration approaches for counselors, therapists, social workers, helping professionals, instructors, and students. Since no two clients (and no two therapists) are the same, we sought to present a model that is both practical and flexible. We suggest the reader utilize the interventions that feel most natural and beneficial, and which best accord with the therapist's strengths and the client's needs. With use, we believe that the models suggested here will both yield positive therapeutic results for the client and serve as the basis for development and improvisation in the hands of the helping professional.

Our approach in developing the model was, first, to undertake a near exhaustive review of the literature on the topic of counseling and spirituality. As we analyzed multiple techniques and interventions, we found ourselves concurring with Tan (1996) that most applications can be categorized as either *implicit* (done within one's self without the client's awareness), or *explicit* (performed outwardly with the client). During the synthesis stage of our analysis, we developed ten strategies for integrating spirituality and religion into counseling and social work. Of these ten strategies, we grouped the four implicit strategies under the acronym FACE and the six explicit strategies using the acronym SPIRIT, thus creating what we called the *FACE-SPIRIT* model.

A special word to instructors: We designed this to be used as a supplemental textbook addressing spirituality in counseling practice. It is short, direct, and easy to read. However, we also designed it to be complete and thorough enough to be used as a stand-alone guide for a class. As the table of contents illustrates, it easy to find sections and chapters dealing with the historical relationship between spirituality and counseling, theories of faith development and spirituality, methods for working with clients' diverse beliefs, spiritual assessment techniques, ethical issues, research findings, references, and of course the specific strategies of the FACE-SPIRT model.

The book also offers helpful vignettes and examples of counselor–client dialogue illustrating each technique. The instructor, therapist, or student will find these invaluable in clarifying the therapeutic concepts and applying them in a real-world setting. Discussion questions are included at the end of each chapter to facilitate classroom dialogue and individual synthetic learning. Finally, a DVD that shows the authors using these techniques with Shawnell and Dale, the clients mentioned in the text, is available for sale through the American Counseling Association (www.counseling.org).

We hope you enjoy our book and find it useful. We believe it is the most complete and pragmatic application available describing how to integrate spirituality into counseling, social work, and other helping relationships. May it serve as a source of inspiration to you and your clients or students.

Acknowledgments

We would like to give a special thanks to Skip Horton-Parker for sharing his invaluable expertise on theology and comparative religious studies, and for his superb editorial assistance. We have appreciated his continuing support from the day we developed the model to the present. We would also like to express our deep gratitude to Stan Love for his warm encouragement and interest in our project, and also to all the staff at Love Publishing for making this book possible. We would especially like to thank Carrie Watterson, Senior Editor, for her dedicated and insightful editing of our manuscript, as well as Vivian Smallwood for her creative design and attention to detail. We are grateful to all of these individuals for their enormous contributions of time, talent, and dedication.

—Radha J. Horton-Parker and R. Charles Fawcett

The *Why, When,* and *How* of Integrating Spirituality Into Counseling and Psychotherapy

All religions, arts and sciences are branches of the same tree. All these aspirations are directed toward ennobling man's life, lifting it from the sphere of mere physical existence and leading the individual towards freedom.

– Albert Einstein

In this initial section of the book, we will explore *why* it is important for helping professionals to integrate spirituality into counseling and psychotherapy. Looking back, we will analyze historical developments in the troubled relationship between spirituality and psychotherapy. Looking forward, we will consider the emerging paradigm, in which spirituality is viewed as being at the core of optimal health and wellness. As part of this discussion, we will compare and contrast the constructs *religion* and *spirituality*.

Next, we will examine *when* spiritual and religious themes are likely to emerge in life. Faith development and life transitions will be emphasized as factors impacting client concerns.

Finally, we will think about *how* to ensure that ethical and competent practice is maintained while incorporating spirituality into helping. We will review the spiritual competencies that are most important for helping professionals to master.

Why Integrate Spirituality Into Counseling and Therapy?

Psychotherapy is the only form of therapy there is.
Since only the mind can be sick, only the mind can be healed.

– Foundation for Inner Peace (1992, p. 1)

There is little question that religion and spirituality are important to most Americans. Eighty-four percent of people living in the United States say religion is important in their lives (Gallup, 2006). An even larger percentage, 86%, attend church on a weekly basis (Gallup). When asked whether they believe in the existence of God, 80% report they are "convinced" God exists, while another 8% state they believe God exists but have a little doubt (Gallup). Additionally, it appears that most Americans consider spirituality to be a key component of their lives (Steen, Engels, & Thweatt, 2006).

People are telling the medical establishment that they want a concern for spirituality to play a part in their health care. For example, 77% of medical patients believe their physicians should take into account their spiritual beliefs (King & Bushwick, 1994). Almost half (48%) of the people surveyed would like their physician to pray with them (King & Bushwick).

The call to integrate spirituality into health care is not limited to the medical realm. Most mental heath clients believe religion and spirituality should also be incorporated in counseling. In one study, 79% of the respondents indicated that it was "important" to address spiritual and religious experiences and values in therapy (Quakenbos, Privette, & Klentz, 1985). In fact, 39% stated they would prefer some form of religious counseling.

In light of such evidence, it is clear that practitioners need to honor their clients' spiritual beliefs, regardless of the therapist's own personal attitudes regarding God, religion, and spirituality. When counselors ignore clients' religious affiliation and values, they are sending them the message that they are irrelevant and thus undermining the therapeutic relationship (Burke et al., 1999). By bracketing the topic of spirituality and making it off limits, therapists make clients uncomfortable about discussing spiritual crises they may be having and make it difficult to engage important existential issues.

Therapists in general tend to be less religious and spiritual than their clients (Bergin & Jensen, 1990). This creates a dilemma for both the therapist and the client, especially if the latter would like to discuss spiritual issues in his or her therapy. It appears that therapists often ignore clients' religious practices or even pathologize them (Ellis, 1991; Gartner, Harmatz, Hohmann, Larson, & Gartner, 1990; Jensen & Bergin, 1988; Myers & Truluck, 1998). We will discuss this issue in greater detail later in the discussion of ethics in chapter 3.

In light of the demonstrated importance of spirituality and religion to clients, it may seem puzzling that therapists have been reluctant to include spirituality in the clinical milieu. We hope to clarify this conundrum through the following examination of the history of spirituality in counseling.

The History of Spirituality in Counseling

The relationship between spirituality and counseling has been a troubled one (Burke et al., 1999). The main difficulty may be found in the attitude of the father of psychotherapy, Sigmund Freud (1928), toward religion. He considered religious doctrines to be pathological:

> Some of them are so improbable, so very incompatible with everything we have laboriously discovered about the reality of the world, that we may compare them—taking adequately into account the psychological differences—to delusions. (p. 55)

He further stated,

> Thus religion would be the universal obsessional neurosis of humanity ... a system of wishful illusions together with a disavowal of reality, such as we find in an isolated form nowhere else but amentia, in a state of blissful hallucinatory confusion. (p. 76)

Historically, many psychoanalysts and therapists have adopted Freud's sentiments. The Freudian judgment of religion as pathological was not limited to early twentieth century theorists, however. Ellis (1991), one of the founders of Cognitive–Behavioral Therapy, vehemently argued that religiosity contributed to mental illness and that atheism was synonymous with mental health. This presupposition has crept into our academic system, where research regarding religious or spiritual health–related issues has become known as the "anti-tenure factor" (Koenig, McCullough, & Larson, 2001, p. 74).

However, not all historically significant psychotherapy theorists have held such antagonistic views towards religion and spirituality. Carl Jung (1933/1962) argued strongly for the importance of spiritual and religious concerns in therapy, a view that contributed to his split with Freud (Cowgil, 1997). Jung contended that the cause of illness in all of his patients over age 35 was being lost spiritually and that true healing could only come from finding that path.

A Paradigm Shift in Psychotherapy

The legacy of Jung's theories undoubtedly played a role in setting the stage for a contemporary renaissance regarding the importance of spirituality in counseling. In the past 15 years there has been a 636% increase in articles about religion and spirituality (Koenig, 2006). In contradistinction to Freud and Ellis, many now hold that spirituality is foundational for mental and physical well-being (Seaward, 1995) and is required for wellness in every other area of our lives (Chandler, Holden, & Kolander, 1992). There has been a shift in health care toward prevention and alternative therapies (Seaward). For example, the authors of the Wheel of Wellness (see Figure 1.1) advocate a model

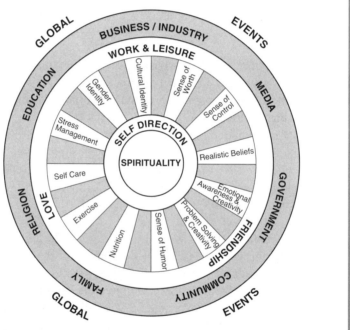

Source: from *"Counseling for wellness: Theory, research, and practice,"* by J. E. Myers and T. J. Sweeney, 2005, Alexandria, VA: ACA, and "Wellness counseling: The evidence base for practice," by J. E. Myers and T. J. Sweeney, 2008, *Journal of Counseling and Development, 86,* pp. 482–493. Reprinted with permission.

THE WHEEL OF WELLNESS

FIGURE 1.1

of health, rather than pathology, and place spirituality at the core of wellness (Myers, Sweeney, & Witmer, 2000).

Mental health care practitioners appear to have made a shift in their awareness, as well. Counselors, social workers, and marriage and family therapists report the perceived importance of religion and values in therapy as significantly higher than do psychologists and psychiatrists (Myers & Truluck, 1998). In all probability this trend will continue, and the salience of spirituality and religion will be recognized increasingly in other fields in the behavioral and health sciences.

The Difference Between Spirituality and Religion

In spite of this sea change in the mental health disciplines, some health care practitioners continue to express ambivalence regarding spirituality and religion. What is the cause of this reticence? Some would trace it to the perceived differences between spirituality and religion (Burke et al., 1999) or to the confusion of spirituality with religion (Myers, Sweeney, & Witmer, 2000; Myers & Truluck, 1998).

To separate and make a clear distinction between spirituality and religion is complicated, as they are fundamentally intertwined. Attempting to define spirituality is especially difficult and runs the danger of excluding personal belief commitments (Cashwell & Young, 2005; Wiggins-Frame, 2005). We have researched scores of definitions for both spirituality and religion, and no two are exactly alike. But before we share some of these definitions, it may be useful to think about your own conceptions of religion and spirituality.

When we speak about religion and spirituality at professional conferences, we like to ask the audience: "What words come into your mind when you hear the word *religion*? Take a moment and think about these. It may be useful to jot them down on a piece of paper. Now, what words do you associate with *spirituality*? Please think about these and write them down. What experiences from your past have shaped these definitions in your mind?"

We are always astonished at the wide range of responses we receive. Some people have positive associations with religion, while others have negative reactions. The same is true with spirituality. Box 1.1 contains common responses culled from our conference experiences.

For our purposes, we define *spirituality* as a set of personal beliefs that transcend the physical and temporal aspects of life that produce a sense of connectedness to the infinite (Myers et al., 2000). It allows individuals to make sense of their daily lives and move toward personal growth and enhanced relationships (Myers & Williard, 2003). *Religion* for our purposes, refers to institutional beliefs and behaviors that are often displayed in a public setting or within a group of participants (Hinterkopf, 1994; Ingersoll, 1994; Myers & Williard). An important distinction is that spirituality is often individual or private while religion is frequently public or in the open.

Empirical Findings Regarding Religiousness and Spirituality

There appears to be growing empirical support associating religion with mental health, physical health, and longevity (George, Ellison, & Larson, 2002; George, Larson, Koenig, & McCullough, 2000; Harrison, Koenig, Hays, Eme-Akwari, & Pargament, 2001; Pargament, 1997). Research in this area has focused on four explanative factors: a) public participation (e.g., religious involvement, services), b) religious

BOX 1.1

Common Words Associated With Religion

| formality | structure | beauty | dogma | peace |
| relationships | traditions | guilt | rules | support |

Common Words Associated With Spirituality

| love | higher power | source | alone | freedom |
| tranquility | isolation | cults | center | wellness |

affiliation, c) religious practices (e.g., meditation, prayer), and d) religious coping (George, Ellison, & Larson). Of these, public participation and religious coping have demonstrated the most significance.

Religious involvement, much like religious public participation, has been associated with improved physical and mental health and longevity (George, Ellison, & Larson, 2002). In a meta-analytic review, researchers analyzed 42 independent studies comparing religious involvement that included religious attendance, membership, finding strength and comfort in one's religion, and mortality (McCullough, Hoyt, Larson, Koenig, & Thoresen, 2000). The studies compared religious involvement and included follow-up measures for surviving respondents. The results indicated that people who measured higher in religious involvement had 129% greater likelihood of survival than those who scored lower on those same measures (McCullough et al.).

Religious coping—which includes active and passive methods of turning to religion and spirituality in times of distress—appears to have a larger impact on physical, psychological, and spiritual outcomes than global measures of religiousness (Pargament, Koenig, Tarakeshwar, & Hahn, 2004). Examples of religious coping can be both positive and negative and can be seen in Table 1.1. Numerous researchers have examined this construct and found that positive religious coping is associated with quality of life in patients with cancer (Tarakeshwar et al., 2006), less distress following cardiac surgery (Ai, Park, Huang, Rodgers, & Tice, 2007), lower self-reports of psychiatric symptoms in young adults with

TABLE 1.1	EXAMPLES OF POSITIVE AND NEGATIVE RELIGIOUS COPING	
	Positive Religious Coping	*Negative Religious Coping*
	Seeking spiritual support	Passive religious deferral
	Religious forgiveness	Punishing reappraisal
	Active religious surrender	Marking religious boundaries
	Religious conversion	Demonic reappraisal
	Seeking religious direction	Spiritual discontent
	Religious purification	Self-directed religious coping

serious mental illness (Phillips & Stein, 2007), and buffered effects of negative life events in adult Protestant church members (Bjorck & Thurman, 2007). In a two-year longitudinal study, researchers associated positive religious coping methods in medically ill elderly patients with frequently improved physical and cognitive functioning, lowered levels of depression, and increased spiritual outcomes (i.e., closeness to God, church attendance, and spiritual growth) (Pargament et al., 2004).

Other studies have found negative or mixed results regarding religious coping and other religious variables. In a nine month follow-up of patients from a London hospital visit, it was found that those with stronger religious beliefs were more likely to have poorer outcomes than their less religious counterparts (King, Speck, & Thomas, 1999). In a study of college students, religious coping was found to have non-statistical significance in relation to depression and anxiety (Hovey & Seligman, 2007). In a qualitative study, it appeared that religious phenomena (beliefs, experiences, rituals, etc.) were associated with higher levels of depression and anxiety in men who lost their partner to AIDS (Richards & Folkman, 1997). Using a large Canadian National Health survey, researchers found church attendance associated with lower levels of depression (Baetz, Griffin, Bowen, Koenig, Marcoux, 2004). However, the authors were unable to explain why those who reported the importance of spirituality/religion had higher rates of depression. Others have found that religious factors in unwed teenage mothers, particularly Catholics with frequent church attendance, were associated with high depression levels (Sorenson, Grindstaff, & Turner, 1995). Guilt and shame associated with the stress of being unwed mothers were factors that might explain these findings.

Until recently, spirituality received little attention in the research literature (Young, Cashwell, & Shcherbakova, 2000). However, current research has revealed the positive associations related to spirituality or spiritual well-being. In a study of people living with leukemia, a strong relationship was found between spiritual well-being and quality of life (O'Connor, Guilfoyle, Breen, Mukhardt, & Fisher, 2007). Others have suggested that spirituality is associated with healthy behaviors in African American college students (Bowen Reid & Smalls, 2004). In addition, spiritual wellness has been found to have an inverse relationship with depression in adolescents, college under-graduates, midlife adults, and older adults (Briggs & Shoffner, 2006; Wong, Rew, & Slaikeu, 2006; Young et al.).

The relationship between spirituality and anxiety is more tenuous. Although spirituality has been found to serve as a buffer between nega-tive life events and anxiety (Young et al., 2000), it has also been associ-ated with higher stress and greater levels of premenstrual symptomology (Lustyk, Beam, Miller, & Olson, 2006). In a sample of college students, spirituality was found to be positively related to perceived stress and anger (Winterowd, Harrist, Thomason, Worth, & Carlozzi, 2005).

Although religious involvement, religious coping, and spirituality may be clearly helpful for many people, some research suggests that such practices are neutral or even harmful for certain individuals. Thus, as helping professionals, we must attempt to understand our clients' unique needs, eliminate our own biases (as much as possible), and work toward their best interests and overall wellness.

Summary

Most Americans consider religion to be important in their lives and expect their spiritual needs to be addressed in their overall health care. While therapists were once reluctant to integrate spirituality into coun-seling, a new paradigm has emerged in which spirituality is recognized as an essential component of wellness and worthy of therapeutic atten-tion. Although distinctions are made between "spirituality" and "reli-gion," empirical research findings suggest that both constructs are associated with mental and physical health and longevity.

Discussion Questions

Below are questions you may wish to ask yourself (or, if you are in a group, discuss together). You might also find it helpful to write down your thoughts as you reflect on these questions.

1. What roles have spirituality and religion played in your life?

2. In your opinion, how are spirituality and religion related? Can they be separated, or are they intrinsic to one another?
3. What words would you associate with *spirituality* and *religion?* (see Box 1.1 above.)
4. How might your views, as expressed above, influence your work with clients?
5. Are there particular religious or spiritual views you might feel comfortable in addressing? If so, what are they? Why?
6. Are there religious or spiritual perspectives that might make you uncomfortable? If so, what are they? Why?
7. If you have had experience as a helping professional:

   a. What has been your experience in discussing religion and spirituality with your clients?
   b. As you consider your previous clients, have you tended to see religion and/or spirituality as helpful or harmful to them? Give examples.

When to Integrate Spirituality Into Counseling and Psychotherapy

The personal life deeply lived always expands into truths beyond itself.

– Anais Nin

In the Introduction, we discussed the importance of integrating spirituality into helping, and now we turn to recognizing and addressing spiritual and religious issues when they emerge in our work with clients. In this chapter, we will consider various times and situations in which spiritual and religious issues may become especially salient in individuals' lives, how these concerns can be broached in the therapeutic context, and how spirituality can serve as a means of healing.

Before we begin, here are some questions to ponder:

- Can you think of times in your own life when the need for religion or spirituality came to the forefront of your awareness?
- If so, what was going on in your life, and what roles did religion or spirituality play?
- How was your life impacted by these experiences?

In leading workshops, we often ask participants about their own experiences involving religion or spirituality, and we typically receive a variety of responses. While some individuals report that religion or spirituality has had an especially major impact in times of crises, others reveal that they cannot think of a single moment when spirituality has *not* been important to them. We receive a plethora of responses regarding whether experiences of religion and spirituality have been positive or negative, ranging from supreme solace to tremendous guilt. Most agree, however, that religion and spirituality can significantly impact us throughout life.

Fowler's Theory of the Development of Faith

James Fowler (1981) suggested that spirituality develops in stages as we go through life, much as cognitive and moral development does. In his model, spiritual development is a normal part of human experience. According to Fowler, throughout life, individuals are faced with *ontological* concerns—that is, issues pertaining to ultimate reality. Individuals often formulate and answer these questions differently at various stages of life. Thus, a young child may wonder if a beloved family pet will go to heaven and be with Grandma, while an older adult may ponder the gravity of having "lust in one's heart" or of committing sins of omission. James Fowler's empirical studies of how individuals grasp basic meaning when presented with existential questions led to his model of faith development. It is important to note that Fowler does not use the term *faith* to refer to a particular belief or religion, but rather to trust in and loyalty to a transcendent center of value and power.

In his model, Fowler (1981) proposed that faith development is closely related to psychosocial development and that it occurs in stages similar to the cognitive and moral developmental stages of Piaget and Kohlberg. Fowler's structural–developmental model of faith development includes the following assumptions:

1. The potential to develop faith is a universal capacity that all individuals possess from birth.

2. The stages of faith are hierarchical, with the latter stages building upon previous stages.
3. Not all individuals reach all stages.

Fowler believed that all humans have the innate ability to develop faith from the moment of birth. This capacity for faith development is present in all people across all cultures. Whether an individual develops faith, however, depends upon his or her environment and social interactions. Faith is shaped by community, language, ritual, nurture, and human experience, as well as by transcendent forces.

In this model, the stages of faith are hierarchical, with the latter stages building upon previous stages. Fowler (1981) describes faith development as occurring in a spiraling pattern in which each subsequent stage

> marks the rise of a new set of capacities or strengths in faith. These add to and reconceptualize previous patterns of strength without negating or supplanting them. Certain life issues with which faith must deal recur at each stage; hence the spiral movements in part overlap each other, though each successive stage addresses these issues at a new level of complexity. (p. 274)

Fowler contends that progression through the stages represents a broadening of vision, valuing, and depth of selfhood, allowing individuals to have increased intimacy with others, themselves, and the world.

Not all individuals reach the higher stages, however, and some adults never move out of the stages of childhood or adolescence. Movement from one stage to the next can be painful and protracted, and individuals can get stuck in any of the stages. Arrested development is especially likely to occur if individuals are not in a given stage at the right time for their lives, as each stage has "its proper time of ascendancy" (Fowler, 1981, p. 274). Fowler's stages of faith are presented in Table 2-1.

Pre-stage: Undifferentiated

In this model, Pre-stage: Undifferentiated faith occurs in infancy and corresponds to Erikson's psychosocial crisis of trust versus mistrust.

TABLE 2.1

FOWLER'S STAGES OF FAITH DEVELOPMENT

Stage	*Age*	*Characteristics*
Pre-stage: Undifferentiated faith	Infancy	Foundation for later faith development Seeds of trust, hope, and courage compete with fears of abandonment
Stage 1: Intuitive-Projective faith	Early Childhood	Self-awareness emerges Intuition guides grasp of relationship to ultimate reality Imagination fills in conceptual gaps in understanding Terrifying fantasies of death and sex may arise from limited knowledge and misconceptions about society's cultural taboos
Stage 2: Mythic-Literal faith	Middle Childhood	Reality is interpreted literally Symbols are one-dimensional Rules are considered to be real and concrete Ultimate reality is understood through anthropomorphic characters in cosmic stories
Stage 3: Synthetic-Conventional faith	Adolescence	Ultimate reality is structured in inter-personal terms with images of unifying value and power derived from qualities experienced in personal relationships Beliefs are those of the dominant group Personal identity is rooted in belonging to the group
Stage 4: Individuative-Reflective faith	Young adulthood	Self identity and world view become more differentiated from others Own interpretations of ultimate reality are formed Critical reflection and awareness of complexity of life arises

(continued)

Stage	Age	Characteristics
Stage 4: *(cont.)*		Disillusionment with previous beliefs may occur
Stage 5: Conjunctive faith	Midlife and beyond	Unrecognized issues from past become integrated into self Past is reclaimed and reworked to arrive at new meaning and deeper awareness Heightened spiritual revelations are possible
Stage 6: Universalizing faith	Rarely achieved	Extreme lucidity and compassion May involve martyrdom for faith and being more greatly appreciated after death

Adapted from Fowler as cited in *The unfolding life: Counseling across the lifespan.* (p. 60), by R. J. Horton-Parker & N. W. Brown, 2002, Westport, CT: Bergin & Garvey.

TABLE 2.1 *(continued)*

Infants, who have not yet developed a sense of self separate from others, are totally dependent on their caregivers. If an infant's needs are met in a timely and caring manner, he or she will feel a sense of safety and security that will provide the foundation for the later development of trust and faith. Whenever the infant's perceived needs are not met as quickly or completely as desired, however, a sensed threat of abandonment will emerge that can undermine trust and faith in the years ahead. In this period, which precedes language acquisition, the infant's mutual relationship with his or her primary caregiver shapes his or her pre-image of God. Just as the infant is separate from, but totally dependent on, this immensely powerful "other" who knew and loved him or her from the beginning of consciousness, so will the pre-image of God be one of a benevolent, all-powerful caretaker who will provide love and expect love in return.

Stage 1: Intuitive-Projective faith

As children move into early childhood and acquire language, the first stage of faith begins. Stage 1: Intuitive-Projective faith, which spans the years from 2 to 7, is a time of growing self-awareness and tremendous curiosity about how the world works. Young children ask many "why" questions as they intuitively attempt to understand their relationship to the ultimate conditions of existence. As Piaget described, preoperational thought is characterized by magical and egocentric thinking, so a 4-year-old girl may believe that her misbehavior caused God to make Grandma die. Gaps in children's conceptual understanding are filled in by their imagination as they attempt to understand the world. Children's fantasies may produce terrifying images as they begin to learn about sex, death, and the cultural taboos of society from the important adults in their world. Stories that adults tell children—whether from the Bible or fairy tales—create powerful and long-lasting images that can continue to influence individuals into adulthood. Thus an adult may harbor secret fears of burning in hell that emerge in dreams without being able to rationally identify their source.

Stage 2: Mythic-Literal Faith

Stage 2: Mythic-Literal faith arises in middle childhood during the school years. During this stage, which corresponds to Piaget's concrete operations, children's imaginative grasp of the world yields to a literal interpretation of reality. Children develop their own stories to form a narrative of their lives. Because children cannot yet think abstractly or hypothetically, their symbols are one-dimensional, and they take rules literally. From these rules, children construct a set of moral standards based upon a sense of fairness and reciprocity, so a child might assume, for example, "if you want to go to heaven, you'd better be good all the time." Children understand ultimate reality through cosmic stories and narratives with anthropomorphic characters. Thus a child may consider heaven to be a place in the sky where God lives (and, of course, God has a long, white beard).

Stage 3: Synthetic-Conventional Faith

In adolescence, Stage 3: Synthetic-Conventional faith emerges. As adolescents enter Piaget's stage of formal operations, they become able to think hypothetically and to imagine what is possible, rather than just what exists in the concrete world. It is also at this time that adolescents are attempting to define who they are, and interpersonal relationships become critically important in the process of identity development. Adolescents seek peer approval and define themselves based upon the reactions of their friends as they experiment with new social roles and behaviors. With the ability to think hypothetically, adolescents can imagine and long for relationships in which they can be totally and unconditionally accepted for who they are and that this love can reach inexhaustible depths. Based upon the ideal of a rich and mysterious transcendent love, adolescents structure ultimate reality in interpersonal terms, with images of unifying value and power derived from qualities experienced in their personal relationships. Adolescents' beliefs are strongly influenced by those of the dominant group to which they belong, and their personal identity is rooted in belonging to the group. Because belonging to the group is so critical to adolescents' sense of identity, questioning or criticizing group values is considered a threat to their being and will bring a fierce defense. Many adults never progress beyond this nonanalytical stage and remain unable to question any of the teachings of their faith communities or to tolerate the values of others that differ from their own.

Stage 4: Individuative-Reflective Faith

For those who are able to move beyond the conformity of Synthetic-Conventional faith, Stage 4: Individuative-Reflective faith emerges in young adulthood. Self identity and world view now become more differentiated from others, and individuals form their own interpretations of ultimate reality as they question their earlier assumptions. Critical reflection occurs and disillusionment with previous beliefs may arise as individuals realize that life is more complex than they once assumed. Individuals also question the meanings behind religious symbols and may no longer tacitly accept these symbols as representative of the sacred as they did in the previous stage. Some adults do not reach this stage in young adulthood, but later in their 30s or 40s when they experience changes in primary relationships, such as divorce or the death of parents.

Stage 5: Conjunctive Faith

Stage 5: Conjunctive faith rarely arises before midlife and is often not achieved at all. In this stage, unrecognized or suppressed issues from the individual's past become integrated into his or her self and outlook. The past is reclaimed and reworked to arrive at new meaning and a deeper awareness. An openness to new depths of religious experience makes heightened spiritual revelations possible, and there is an inclusive acceptance of other spiritual traditions.

Stage 6: Universalizing Faith

Stage 6: Universalizing faith is the highest stage in the model and is extremely rare. It is achieved by those who are more lucid, simple, and fully human than others, individuals who tirelessly strive to achieve the ideals of absolute love and justice and transform present reality into transcendent actuality. Their universalizing compassion makes them heedless of their own pain and suffering. Gandhi and Mother Teresa of Calcutta are excellent examples of Universalizing faith. Such self-actualizing individuals sometimes become martyrs for their faith and are often appreciated more after death than before.

Because spirituality is expressed differently by individuals at varying stages, Fowler's model can be quite helpful as we work with clients. Understanding how individuals conceptualize spiritual issues can be instrumental in helping them work through and resolve concerns.

Life Transitions and Spirituality

Although spirituality is always an essential aspect of our human potential, there are times when spirituality may become especially prominent in our awareness. Spiritual and religious issues often arise as individuals face major life transitions. These life changes fall into two categories: normative and nonnormative.

Normative Changes

Normative changes are developmental transitions that arise as individuals move from one life stage to the next. Although normal and expected, these transitions often bring about a change in roles and require making adjustments. Such transitions may initially create a sense of disequilibrium and leave us feeling a little out of balance. Normative transitions—for example, becoming a caregiver for aging parents at midlife—are often accompanied by spiritual and existential concerns, especially if the transition is difficult. Research has found common existential themes emerging in midlife women participating in spirituality groups, including: finding meaning in life, achieving personal growth and self-acceptance, and discovering their place in the universe and connection to God (Geertsma & Cummings, 2004).

Introduction of Shawnell

To illustrate the impact of both normative and nonnormative transitions, we will now introduce two case studies to which we will refer throughout the book. While one client is attempting to cope with a typical, normative transition, the other is facing a nonnormative life-changing event.

The first client, Shawnell, is a 35-year-old African American woman who is married and has two children. One of her presenting concerns is the stress she is experiencing in caring for her elderly mother. In the dialogue that follows, Shawnell explains her frustration in dealing with this tough normative transition:

Therapist: Shawnell, what would you like to talk about today?
Shawnell: It seems that I can't do anything right with Mom. I take her to all of her doctors' appointments, buy her groceries, clean her house, and she still criticizes me constantly. I try so hard to be a good daughter, but it seems like I always fail. Sometimes I wonder why I was ever born.

Therapist: I hear your frustration! It sounds like caregiving for your mom has been extremely stressful for you.

Nonnormative Changes

While normative changes are often very difficult, at least they are predictable. On the other hand, nonnormative changes are random life events that arise without warning. These transitions, which may be positive or negative, cannot be prepared for in advance. An example of a negative nonnormative transition might be a highly traumatic event, such as a debilitating accident, that causes a person to question his or her essential beliefs. The value of integrating spirituality into counseling is evident from research showing the relationship between spirituality and the ability to adapt to negative nonnormative changes. Numerous studies suggest that spirituality may serve as an important factor in coping with negative life events, including chronic or terminal illnesses, sexual assault, and witnessing traumatic events (Brady, Peterman, Fitchett, Mo, & Cella, 1999; Briggs, Apple, & Aydlett, 2004; Kaczorowski, 1989; Landis, 1996; Mickley, Soeken, & Belcher, 1992; Pargament, 1997).

On a more pleasant note, positive nonnormative transitions are sometimes highly fortuitous events—such as winning the lottery or becoming famous—which may still necessitate rearranging our lives and rethinking our priorities. In the second case study, we will consider a positive life-altering circumstance for our second client, Dale, who came to counseling after encountering a nonnormative transition that many of us might envy.

Introduction of Dale

Dale is a 42-year-old gay man who has been with his life partner, Steve, for 15 years. Dale, who had been employed as an accountant for 17 years, suddenly no longer needed to work after inheriting some very lucrative stocks from an elderly relative.

In spite of their wealth, Dale's partner, Steve, decided to continue working as a successful CPA. Dale, on the other hand, chose to leave accounting because he had never particularly enjoyed it. In the following dialogue, Dale describes his situation and his presenting concern.

Therapist: Dale, you indicated that you just inherited a large sum of money?

Dale: Yes, that's why I'm here. Now that Steve and I have more money than we know what to do with, I'll never have to work again. But what does that mean for me? What will I do with myself? Even though I wasn't crazy about my job, now that I don't have it anymore, I feel empty.

Therapist: It sounds like you're really feeling confused about what to do about that void.

Although many of us might imagine that we wouldn't mind having Dale's problem, the inheritance was the catalyst for much of his personal turmoil. Having to rethink his life, set new goals, and manage a completely new set of choices and options was surely producing stress.

Nonnormative transitions, whether negative or positive, are generally more stressful than normative changes and may result in a spiritual or existential crisis. At such times, individuals may be especially inclined to focus on spiritual, religious, or existential issues in counseling and psychotherapy.

Recognizing and Broaching Spiritual and Religious Issues

Both Shawnell and Dale were considering the meaning of their lives as they moved into their new roles. They were questioning how to live honorably in the world and in relation to others. Because spiritual and religious issues can be either directly stated by the client or indirectly implied, however, some therapists may wonder how to recognize and broach the topic of ultimate concerns with their clients.

In the following dialogue, Shawnell directly states a concern related to her Christian beliefs. As you will see, she questions whether she and her therapist will be able to work together effectively.

Therapist:	Now that we've had a chance to talk about some of your concerns, do you have any questions for me?
Shawnell:	Yes. Are you saved? Have you taken the Lord Jesus Christ as your savior?
Therapist:	You are a devout Christian, and you are worried or skeptical of working with a possibly non-Christian therapist.
Shawnell:	Well, yes. I just don't know if I can work with someone who doesn't have strong Christian values.
Therapist:	You don't want someone steering you wrong.
Shawnell:	Yes … and I'm not sure a non-Christian would really understand my perspective.
Therapist:	May I ask you a question?
Shawnell:	Sure.
Therapist:	Do all of the members of your church have the same views or perspectives on different passages of the Bible or interpretations of church doctrines?
Shawnell:	(smiling) Well no … sometimes we get into some pretty heated debates about how to interpret different passages.
Therapist:	I see … but despite some of the differences of perspective, I would imagine you receive a lot of benefit and support from your involvement in your church.
Shawnell:	Oh yes … it has been hugely important and helpful in my life.
Therapist:	Do you think that even if you and I may have different perspectives on spirituality … similar to the various members of your church, that as long as I am sensitive and respectful of your views, we might be able to work together constructively?
Shawnell:	Yes … I suppose so. I hadn't thought of it like that.

In Shawnell's case, the spiritual issues were obvious and needed to be addressed. Such concerns may, however, be covert, indirect, or hidden, as was the case with Dale in the earlier dialogue. His statement about feeling empty offered a clue that deeper spiritual or existential issues were present, even though Dale didn't directly state them.

Mental health professionals may wonder how to work with clients like Dale, who do not express spiritual issues directly. In the next chapter, we will discuss how to work with clients such as Shawnell and Dale who hold differing belief systems. We will also explore ethical responsibilities that must be considered when addressing spiritual and religious issues in counseling and psychotherapy.

Summary

In order to effectively assist clients, helpers need to be sensitive to spiritual and religious themes that may emerge in their work with clients. Issues of faith typically arise over the lifespan and may be expressed in various ways, based upon the developmental level of the client. Major life transitions also often prompt clients to search for meaning in their lives and to seek answers to existential questions. Religious and spiritual concerns, which clients may state either directly or indirectly, must first be recognized and then skillfully addressed by helping professionals to respond to clients' needs.

Discussion Questions

1. At what times in your own experience have spiritual or religious concerns emerged? What was going on in your life, and what roles did religion or spirituality play? How was your life impacted, either negatively or positively, by these experiences?
2. How would you respond to a client who wanted to know which church you attended? Suppose you were of a different faith tradition than the client or were an atheist and never attended church. How would you answer the question?
3. Can you think of any life transitions that might be especially likely to bring forth concerns of a spiritual or religious nature for individuals? Why?

3

An Overview of Spiritual Competencies and Ethical Practice in Integrating Spirituality Into Counseling and Psychotherapy

We are all affecting the world every moment, whether we mean to or not. Our actions and states of mind matter, because we are so deeply interconnected with one another.

– Ram Dass

If spirituality is a core component of wellness, what does it mean to be a spiritually competent helping professional? What standards apply to our work with clients in spiritual and religious domains? To address such questions, in 1997 the Association for Spiritual, Ethical, and Religious Values in Counseling (ASERVIC), a division of the American Counseling Association (ACA), held a Summit on Spirituality. At this groundbreaking event, a comprehensive list of counselor competencies was developed to help insure that spirituality was included in training and practice ("Summit on Spirituality," 1997). In this chapter, we will discuss the competencies, offer guidelines for ethical behavior, and

BOX 3.1

ASERVIC Competencies

Competency 1 – The professional counselor can explain the difference between religion and spirituality, including similarities and differences.

Competency 2 – The professional counselor can describe religious and spiritual beliefs and practices in a cultural context.

Competency 3 – The professional counselor engages in self-exploration of religious and spiritual beliefs in order to increase sensitivity, understanding, and acceptance of diverse belief systems.

Competency 4 – The professional counselor can describe her or his religious and/or spiritual belief system and explain various models of religious or spiritual development across the lifespan.

Competency 5 – The professional counselor can demonstrate sensitivity and acceptance of a variety of religious and/or spiritual expressions in client communication.

Competency 6 – The professional counselor can identify limits of her or his understanding of a client's religious or spiritual expression, demonstrate appropriate referral skills, and generate possible referral sources.

Competency 7 – The professional counselor can assess the relevance of the religious and/or spiritual domains in the client's therapeutic issues.

Competency 8 – The professional counselor is sensitive to and receptive of religious and/or spiritual themes in the counseling process as befits the expressed preference of each client.

Competency 9 – The professional counselor uses a client's religious and/or spiritual beliefs in the pursuit of the client's therapeutic goals as befits the client's expressed preference.

suggest strategies by which helping professionals can assist clients with differing religious and/or spiritual belief systems.

The Spiritual Competencies

Competency 1

The professional counselor can explain the difference between religion and spirituality, including similarities and differences.

As we emphasized in chapter 1, there are both differences and similarities between religion and spirituality. Some clients will make this distinction themselves while others will not. Some clients will contend that they are spiritual but not religious, some will say they are both, and some will assert that they are neither. It is therefore important for helping professionals to realize that although some individuals may believe the two terms to be inextricably intertwined, religion and spirituality have different meanings. As we emphasized previously, we will consider spirituality to be more personal, subjective, and internal to the self, with religion being more institutionalized, objective, and external to the self. Spirituality may not be based on a particular set of formal beliefs practiced in a group setting, as religion usually is. Although we recognize that there are always exceptions to these general assumptions, spirituality can be considered to be independent of any particular denomination or faith tradition and to be a universal human potential.

Competency 2

The professional counselor can describe religious and spiritual beliefs and practices in a cultural context.

While it may seem daunting to attempt to understand all the world's faith traditions in a cultural context, helping professionals can certainly try to educate themselves and acquire as much information as possible. We strongly recommend attending workshops and conferences, taking continuing education classes, and reading the professional literature to keep abreast. Later in this chapter, we will discuss how to begin considering the ways in which culture may influence individuals' beliefs and practices in religious and spiritual domains, so that you may embark upon your own quest to develop greater multicultural literacy.

Competency 3

The professional counselor engages in self-exploration of religious and spiritual beliefs in order to increase sensitivity, understanding, and acceptance of diverse belief systems.

Without understanding ourselves, it is difficult to imagine helping others, so it is crucial for helping professionals to be continually engaged in spiritual self-exploration and growth. If we fail to focus on this core area of wellness in ourselves, how can we hope to assist others? We believe that the more we learn about the role of religious and spiritual beliefs and practices in our own lives, as well as in those of others, the greater sensitivity, acceptance, and tolerance we will have for diverse traditions. In chapters 5–8, we will discuss strategies that helping professionals can use to incorporate their own spirituality into their work with clients, and we will offer additional opportunities for self-exploration throughout the book.

Competency 4

The professional counselor can describe her or his religious and/or spiritual belief system and explain various models of religious or spiritual development across the lifespan.

According to James Fowler (1981), faith development arises in stages, similar to cognitive, social, and moral development. Other theorists emphasize the many life transitions that may impact religious and spiritual development across the lifespan. We presented a detailed discussion of Fowler's stages and life transitions in chapter 2.

Competency 5

The professional counselor can demonstrate sensitivity and acceptance of a variety of religious and/or spiritual expressions in client communication.

Our clients offer us many clues regarding what they may need to find lasting fulfillment and who they are at their deepest levels. As helpers, however, we must be perceptive enough to recognize the true gifts that we are offered through our clients' disclosures. Often they give us only fleeting glimpses of their innermost selves, and it is up to us to assure them total safety and security if we seek to know more. Because religious and spiritual values comprise the very core of many individuals' existence, we can expect them to be closely guarded. As helping professionals, we must demonstrate great sensitivity and acceptance of our clients' beliefs if we desire to be of service. From the client who speaks of astral projection to the one who is slain by the holy spirit, we must honor the meaning that such experiences hold and allow the client to explore their significance. Chapter 8 shows how Existential Empathy can be used to enhance our ability to be the safe haven that our clients need for growth to occur.

Competency 6

The professional counselor can identify limits of her or his understanding of a client's religious or spiritual expression, demonstrate appropriate referral skills, and generate possible referral sources.

Regardless of how sincerely we may wish to help, some issues are beyond our ability to address. Although our clients may not realize that we are exceeding our level of competence, we must know our own limits and be willing to make necessary referrals. In the next section of this chapter, we will discuss how to work with clients who have differing beliefs and how to find appropriate referral sources.

Competency 7

The professional counselor can assess the relevance of the religious and/or spiritual domains in the client's therapeutic issues.

In order to understand the role of spirituality and/or religion in our clients' lives, we can perform a spiritual assessment, which will be discussed in chapter 4. Simple procedures, which may begin at intake and continue after counseling has begun, can help us to uncover the relevance of spirituality and religion to our clients' issues.

For many clients, the faith and fellowship gained from being a member of a religious tradition or spiritual community can be a tremendous source of support that facilitates healing. It is important to realize, however, that misinterpreted and misapplied religious or spiritual beliefs and practices may contribute to clients' difficulties. For example, consider a diabetic client who attempts to undertake a religious fast by going all day without eating, even though her work performance is compromised by her dizzy spells. In Box 3.2, you'll see another example of how mistaken or misunderstood religious beliefs may negatively impact a client.

BOX 3.2

"Have Faith"

I (Charlie) am working with a client who is deeply spiritual. She practices yoga, meditates twice a day, and is a member of a like-minded spiritual community. The friendships and activities she participates in with her fellow seekers have been a great source of support for her, especially last year during a severe bout with depression. At that time, she came into counseling with a bipolar diagnosis and after a few months of treatment, medication, and support from her church, she left therapy. Indeed, she felt so well that she stopped taking her medications. Six months later she returned to therapy. She was drowning in financial debt due to having leased a home that cost twice what she could afford. The client stated that her friends from the "prosperity course" at her church had encouraged her to lease the house and to believe that if she had enough faith, "the universe would manifest the money." While we may have great respect for the truth and helpfulness of religious beliefs, such precepts can be misinterpreted and abused, thus harming rather than helping clients.

Competency 8

The professional counselor is sensitive to and receptive of religious and/or spiritual themes in the counseling process as befits the expressed preference of each client.

By doing a spiritual assessment, we become aware of our clients' religious and/or spiritual preferences. Being truly receptive to their spiritual or religious themes, however, requires much more. We must be still and focused, have compassion, listen deeply and empathically, and genuinely care. We believe that such abilities are made possible only through working on ourselves, and that is why the inner part of our FACE-SPIRIT model highlights strategies that involve the implicit integration of spirituality into counseling. An overview of these techniques will be presented in chapter 4 and will be further elucidated in chapters 5–8.

Competency 9

The professional counselor uses a client's religious and/or spiritual beliefs in the pursuit of the client's therapeutic goals as befits the client's expressed preference.

In addition to implicitly integrating spirituality into counseling and therapy, it may occasionally be beneficial to use more explicit interventions to help our clients. Based upon the results of their spiritual assessments, clients' therapeutic goals may sometimes be best served by reflecting their religious and/or spiritual orientations. To help clients accomplish their goals, the outer portion of our FACE-SPIRIT model, which will be introduced in chapter 4, can be used. Detailed illustrations of the strategies for explicit integration will be provided in chapters 9–14.

Working With Diverse Beliefs

Helping professionals may wonder how to work with the vast diversity of religious and spiritual beliefs and practices, especially if they are unfamiliar with the clients' religious or spiritual path. Don't be afraid to ask questions about what you don't know. In fact, adopting a stance of not-knowing is often a highly productive means of discovering more about clients' spirituality. For example, therapists can ask clients to share their beliefs about the etiology of their distress, as well as what they might consider to be the best means to alleviate it—which may include spirituality (Jones et al., 2001). Doing this can help to reveal whether clients associate their issues with spirituality. For example, a client might say, "This suffering is my karma for doing something wrong," or "God is punishing me for having impure thoughts, and I need to repent."

Likewise, some clients may believe that certain spiritual interventions would be helpful in resolving their issues, such as prayer, meditation, and scripture reading (Constantine, Myers, Kindaichi, & Moore, 2004). It can be beneficial to join forces collaboratively with clients in the selection of such interventions. For example, a therapist might suggest homework assignments like keeping a prayer journal or attend-ing a meditation group. Mental health professionals may also wish to discuss with clients the in-session religious behaviors the clients may desire and expect to be present in counseling, such as a conservative Christian client who prefers that each session begin with a devotional reading or prayer (Belaire & Young, 2002). These interventions would be based on the clients' own needs and desires, rather than the spiritual inclinations of the counselor, and they must be strategies that are com-fortable for both client and therapist.

It can be efficacious to create alliances that involve both clients and their priests, pastors, rabbis, imams, or indigenous spiritual leaders (Constantine et al., 2004). It may also be helpful to form collaborative relationships with pastoral counselors, religious studies experts, and clergypersons interested in counseling. If appropriate, counselors may wish to seek the assistance of pastoral counselors, family members, and others within the clients' spiritual community to aid in treatment. In some cases, clients may even appreciate being allowed to invite these individuals to participate in their counseling sessions (Jones et al., 2001). In other cases, clients may be referred to "friendly clergy" from various faith traditions for additional help outside of therapy (Faiver, O'Brien, & McNally, 1998). Through such collaborations, specific spiritual interventions (e.g., faith healing, prayer, and music) can some-times be incorporated into the client's treatment plan (Adksion-Bradley, Johnson, Sanders, Duncan, & Holcomb-McCoy, 2005). For example, within the African American community, the Black church serves as an invaluable source of strength and healing. Black pastors, who often have tremendous influence on their congregations, can be very instrumental in helping to bring about desired changes in their parishioners' lives.

There is a lot to learn and counselors need to be open to beliefs that are different from their own. It is critical that therapists maintain an attitude of openness and avoid imposing their own personal values in counseling. Sometimes this can occur inadvertently as a result of a lack of familiarity with the beliefs and practices of other religions and cultures, so it is important to learn about the variety of customs and expressions of spirituality.

For example, the counselor should take into consideration whether the client is from a culture that is individualistic (as in western cultures) or collectivist in its thinking, as is generally true of traditional eastern cultures. This differentiation can help the counselor tailor an approach to the worldview of the client. Also, a counselor should consider the types of spiritual presuppositions and praxis valued in the client's religion. Examples might include culture-specific attitudes regarding elders or parents; the importance of spiritual disciplines such as meditation, fasting, or prayer; or concepts such as karma, scriptural inerrancy, or being filled with the Holy Spirit. If the counselor understands the worldview of the client within his or her cultural context, it becomes much easier to grasp the issues with which the client may be struggling. For example, consider the Fundamentalist Protestant Christian (FPC) woman who believes she cannot leave her abusive spouse because "wives must submit to their husbands." Her reluctance to get out of a potentially dangerous situation can only be fully apprehended by realizing that FPC families typically involve male headship and a hierarchical power structure, in which the husband provides leadership and the wife is expected to be submissive to his leadership (Foss & Warnke, 2003). Without an understanding of these beliefs, it would be very difficult to fathom the complexity of the client's dilemma.

Mental health professionals are encouraged to periodically conduct a self-inventory of their own worldviews and spiritual beliefs and to strive to become aware of their own biases. A good way to do this is to engage in interreligious dialogue and proactively seek information about other practices and beliefs. It can be especially helpful to develop a network of clergypersons from a variety of faith traditions to ask specific questions concerning assumptions and scriptural interpretations within their communities. Of course, all of these activities should be considered ongoing processes to be continued throughout the helper's professional life.

Vignettes

As an example of spiritually diverse beliefs, consider the following statements of our two clients: Shawnell and Dale. In the first, Shawnell describes an experience she had one morning in church; in the second, Dale expands upon a late-night occurrence of astral projection he had at home:

Shawnell: Oh, it was incredible! The Holy Spirit fell on the meeting, and before I knew what had hit me, I was on the floor, flat on my back, for 20 minutes! I was so blessed to feel God's presence!

Dale: I was floating above the bed, and I looked down, and saw Steve and me sleeping so peacefully in each other's arms. After all the stress we've been facing lately, I can't describe what a sense of serenity that gave me. I then felt confident that together we could handle anything that came our way.

Both experiences were intensely powerful and immensely meaningful for each of the respective individuals, but they are as different as they were potent. Without adequate knowledge of the varieties of religious experience, it is easy to imagine how these expressions of spirituality could be misconstrued by well-intentioned helping professionals.

Discussion Questions

1. What might your immediate reactions be if you heard clients speak about such occurrences? How would you respond to each?
2. Considered within the context of the client's belief system, what might such experiences mean?
3. Have you encountered other types of extraordinary spiritual experiences with your clients? What significance did they have in the therapeutic process?

Ethical Considerations

Remember the old adage about the road to hell being paved with good intentions? In any discussion of the integration of spirituality into counseling, first and foremost we must emphasize the caveat that helpers are to avoid imposing their values on clients (ACA, 2005). We are tempted to assume that we have the one "true" religion and that clients will surely be helped by partaking of the "salvation" which we have found and desire to share. Although such inclinations may be well-intended, they have no place in helping. We must vigorously resist the proclivity to proselytize and allow our clients to find their own way.

Basing our interventions on the client's spiritual assessment can help to insure that we act in a manner congruent with our client's values, rather than impose our own values. For example, if the client's spiritual assessment reveals that he or she is a devout Evangelical Christian, we may feel confident that he or she would feel comfortable with, and might even expect, prayer to be part of counseling. In this case, asking the client if he or she would like to begin the session with a short prayer might not be inappropriate. On the other hand, if we are unsure of the client's spiritual orientation, it would be better to wait and see if the client asks to pray in a session, rather than suggesting it ourselves. When uncertain of whether to use a direct specific intervention, we recommend asking the question, "Whose needs would be met by using this strategy?" If we find that we are attempting to meet our own needs, rather than those of our client, we should resist the urge to

BOX 3.3

Ethical Considerations

■ Avoid imposing your values on clients.

■ Base your interventions upon the client's spiritual assessment.

■ Ensure you have adequate training for your approach.

■ Maintain the separation of church and state.

■ Avoid dual relationships with clients.

■ Work on your own spiritual development.

■ If you are uncomfortable with explicit spiritual integration strategies, use implicit spiritual interventions engage in a behavior that has the potential to damage the relationship and make the client uncomfortable.

Helpers must insure that they have adequate training before attempting to work with religious or spiritual issues (ACA, 2005). Therapists should carefully consider whether a direct spiritual intervention is appropriate, especially for severely disturbed clients. If a helper lacks the necessary knowledge or skills to deal with the religious or spiritual issues of his or her client, a referral should be considered.

Mental health professionals should avoid violating laws governing the separation of church and state. For example, it may be inappropriate to use explicit spiritual interventions, such as meditation, with children in school settings. It is also important to avoid allowing boundaries to become blurred or to create a dual relationship (e.g., being both a therapist and spiritual director). Although we may feel flattered if our clients consider us to be great spiritual gurus, we must guard against such potential transference and address it if it occurs.

Additionally, helping professionals should not attempt to assist others without working on their own spiritual development (Genia, 2000). We strongly encourage helpers to periodically assess their own levels of wellness, while paying particular attention to the spiritual domain.

If for any reason, the helper feels uncomfortable or worries that it may be unethical to explicitly integrate spirituality with the client, he or she can still use the inner part of our model, the implicit interventions, without the client ever knowing it. Remember that, as helping professionals, it is always possible for us to work on our own spiritual development. We have the freedom to change and to grow in love at all times. It is never too early or too late to begin our own inner journey, and it will only enhance our ability to help others.

Finally, if you are uncertain as to whether a practice or intervention is ethical, consult another counselor or health care provider who is familiar with your professional code of ethics (ACA, 2005). The extra perspective from your colleague(s) may enhance your understanding of the situation and possibly help you rethink any questionable aspects of your approach. Alternatively, feedback from another professional may provide a rationale and support if your practices are brought into question later by a convening authority.

Summary

ASERVIC's Spiritual Competencies—which will be discussed in greater detail throughout the book—provide guidelines for ensuring that spirituality is incorporated effectively into practice in the helping professions. By being mindful of the spiritual competencies, practitioners can more efficaciously strive to meet the unique needs of their clients and facilitate their overall wellness. Ethical practice necessitates that helping professionals periodically assess and work on their own spiritual development, assess the spiritual needs of their clients, and refrain from imposing their views on clients. In addition, helping professionals are advised to avoid dual relationships, respect the separation between church and state, continually seek training, and consult with others regarding the appropriateness of specific spiritual interventions with clients.

Discussion Questions

1. Can you think of any examples of clients' spiritual or religious issues that might be beyond your level of competence to address? What would make these issues so problematic for you, and how might you deal with them?
2. If you were asked to articulate your own most essential core spiritual or religious beliefs, what might they be? How do your convictions influence your view of the world and your interactions with other people?
3. What commonalities do you think might exist in the various religious traditions? How might these common beliefs and/or practices serve as a bridge to understanding others different than yourself?
4. Suppose you had a client who was exhibiting what you considered to be self-defeating or destructive beliefs or behaviors based upon his or her religious convictions. Can you think of any specific examples that might fall into this category? What would you do?

5. During your first session together, your client asks if you have been saved and accepted Jesus Christ as your lord and savior. Suppose you are of a different faith tradition than the client, how might you respond?

How to Integrate Spirituality Into Counseling and Therapy: The FACE-SPIRIT Model

*Sometimes people get the mistaken notion that spirituality is
a separate department of life, the penthouse of existence.
But rightly understood, it is a vital awareness that pervades
all realms of our being.*

– David Steindl-Rast

Despite a growing desire to integrate religion and spirituality into counseling, there is a dearth of curricula and coursework available to train therapists in how to do so (Briggs & Rayle, 2005; Burke et al., 1999; Kelly, 1994, 1995; Myers & Williard, 2003; O'Connor, 2004; Pate & Hall, 2005). Counselors in training often feel inadequate or ill-prepared to broach spirituality-related issues in counseling (Souza, 2002). The remainder of this book is therefore directed toward sharing specifics about how to integrate spirituality into psychotherapy and counseling.

In this chapter we are going to show how the FACE-SPIRIT model can be used to integrate spirituality into helping. In addition, we will discuss how to conceptualize implicit and explicit counseling strategies using the FACE-SPIRIT model and how to conduct a religious/spiritual assessment.

The FACE-SPIRIT Model

We developed the FACE-SPIRIT model to provide therapists and human services workers with a range of strategies that can be used to facilitate counseling for spiritual and religious issues from the perspectives of both the helping professional and the client. While 95% of therapists believe there is a relationship between mental health and spirituality, only 68% of therapists believe it is appropriate to discuss spirituality with their clients (Carlson, Kirkpatrick, Hecker, & Killmer, 2002). This discrepancy has been attributed to a lack of available training regarding effective counseling strategies (Carlson et al.). The FACE-SPIRIT model, with its specific implicit and explicit strategies, bridges this gap and provides therapists with the resources and skills they need to confidently and effectively incorporate spirituality into their practice.

Implicit Integration: FACE

Implicit integration of spirituality in therapy refers to the use of religious or spiritual techniques that are performed without clients' awareness (Tan, 1996, 2000). These covert strategies include practices that the helping professional conducts within himself or herself, often before clients arrive. In our model, these strategies constitute the inner circle (see Figure 4.1). The acronym *FACE* stands for the following strategies:

> **F**ocusing on the present
> **A**sking for guidance
> **C**ompassion cultivation
> **E**xistential empathy

These interventions are discussed in detail in chapters 5 through 8.

Helping professionals can avail themselves of the positive benefits of their own religious or spiritual values and principles without in any way violating their clients' beliefs (Tan, 1996). Implicit strategies are not subject to the ethical concerns that accompany explicit interventions. For example, in settings such as public schools or government agencies, explicit integration of spirituality may collide with concerns

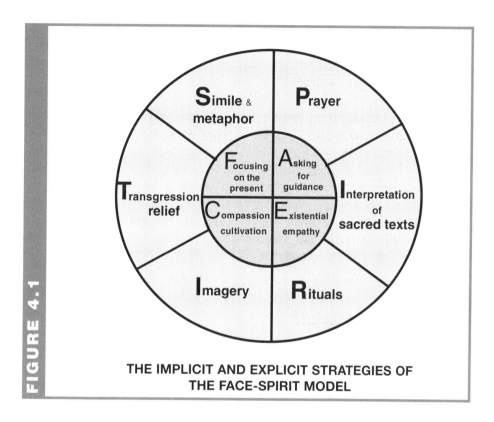

THE IMPLICIT AND EXPLICIT STRATEGIES OF THE FACE-SPIRIT MODEL

regarding the separation of church and state. Implicit integration, however, is always acceptable.

Explicit Integration: SPIRIT

The explicit integration of spirituality into psychotherapy involves openly and directly addressing clients' spiritual and religious issues as part of the therapeutic process (Tan, 1996; 2000). Explicit strategies can be used with clients during sessions or assigned as homework. The acronym *SPIRIT* represents the following explicit interventions, which are located in the outer ring of the FACE-SPIRIT model (Figure 4.1):

> **S**imile and metaphor
> **P**rayer

Interpretation of sacred texts
Rituals
Imagery
Transgression relief

Therapists are not required to be religious or spiritual to utilize explicit integration strategies (Tan, 1996). They do, however, need to be open, sensitive, and respectful of their clients' spiritual and religious beliefs.

Unlike implicit strategies, explicit strategies warrant ethical consideration before use (Genia, 2000; Tan, 1994; Weld & Eriksen, 2007). This book contains information elucidating ethical practice guidelines for ensuring that explicit strategies are used appropriately. The explicit SPIRIT strategies and associated ethical considerations will be discussed in detail in chapters 9–14.

Spiritual Assessment

As with any aspect of counseling, an initial assessment of client problems is required before proper treatment can begin. However, therapists are frequently reluctant to ask about their clients' spiritual lives (Genia, 2000). This is unfortunate, because such assessment is vital to determine whether

- religious and spiritual concerns contribute to clients' presenting problems (Frame, 2003; Kelly, 1995; Richards & Bergin, 2005);
- spirituality and religion are a source of support for clients (Richards & Bergin);
- explicit spiritual interventions would be beneficial (Richards & Bergin) (see chapters 9–14); and
- unresolved spiritual concerns, issues, or doubts need to be addressed (Richards & Bergin).

It is important to understand your therapeutic role, however, and realize that you are not there to serve as a spiritual or religious director

(Frame). If that is what clients are seeking, they should be referred to a clergyperson or spiritual counselor.

A variety of assessment techniques gather spiritual and religious information from clients, but therapists must choose to use them. Available approaches include the use of intake forms, client interviews, spiritual genograms, spirituality timelines, and formal instrumentation.

Intake Forms

An intake form can provide a straightforward means of gathering spiritual and religious information (Frame, 2003; Kelly, 1995; Miller, 2003). Before initially meeting with a therapist, many agencies require clients to complete intake forms that record demographic information, presenting problem(s), family history, medical history, psychological history, substance use, and other pertinent details. Such intake forms can be modified to include questions regarding clients' religious and spiritual histories, current spiritual and religious practices, and any positive or negative issues associated with religious or spiritual concerns. Intake forms offer a quick means of getting an initial glimpse of clients' spirituality. Such topics can be explored in greater detail during the interview process.

Interviews

The intake interview or early sessions are ideal contexts in which to begin to learn about clients' religious and spiritual beliefs, attitudes, and practices. You can ask closed-ended questions to gain specific information, for example, "What is your religion?" Or you can use open-ended leads to elicit broader and more in-depth responses, such as, "Tell me about the role, if any, that religion played in your life while you were growing up."

Here are some initial questions that you might find helpful in an initial interview:

- Do you currently go to a church, synagogue, temple, or mosque? If so, what is its name and/or denomination?
- How frequently do you attend? (Griffith & Griggs, 2001)

■ Tell me about your religious and spiritual beliefs.

■ What role, if any, did religion play in your childhood?

■ What benefits do you receive from your spiritual and religious practices?

■ Do you have any spiritual or religious practices that seem to affect your problem(s)? (Magaletta & Brawer, 1998)

■ Have there been times in your life that you doubted or questioned your religious beliefs? (Griffith & Griggs)

■ Do you use prayer or meditation to help you deal with problems? (Magaletta & Brawer)

■ What is your partner's (if applicable) religious and spiritual views? How does this affect your interaction with him or her? (Griffith & Griggs)

■ On a scale of 0–10, with 0 being *not at all important*, and 10 being *extremely important*, how would you rate the importance of your religious or spiritual beliefs and practices? (Griffith & Griggs)

As with all psychotherapy, maintaining a nonjudgmental and accepting attitude is essential when collecting religious and spiritual information. If you are unsure about the meaning of a specific religious doctrine or practice, ask the client to explain it to you. It is important to remember that religious terms can have varied connotations. For example, you might have two clients who profess to be Christians. However, one may attend a liberal Metropolitan Community Church occasionally, while the other might attend a fundamentalist independent Baptist church two or three times a week. These two clients' beliefs may be radically different (Frame, 2003).

Spiritual Genograms

Another method for assessing clients' religious and spiritual histories is the spiritual genogram (Frame, 2003; Genia, 2000; Miller, 2003). A genogram is similar to a family tree and includes information such as the family's history of physical and mental illnesses, substance use, relationships, ethnic diversity, and religious affiliation (Neukrug &

Fawcett, 2009). A spiritual genogram's primary focus is religion and spirituality. Genograms use a series of symbols and lines representing family members and their relationships. Figure 4.2 illustrates the common symbols used in constructing a genogram (Neukrug & Fawcett).

Although the therapist often constructs the genogram, you can also ask clients to draw one during a session or as homework. The genogram itself provides limited information, but the discussion that accompanies its construction and exploration is often invaluable in gaining useful client information. Figure 4.3 shows a genogram for Shawnell, a client from our vignettes.

Spirituality Timeline

The spirituality timeline is another visual strategy for understanding clients. This tool allows therapists and clients to assess negative and positive life events that have impacted the clients' faith. *Peak, pit,* and *plateau* experiences can be recorded and situated within the context of clients' life stories (Canda & Furman, 1999). Life events are sometimes

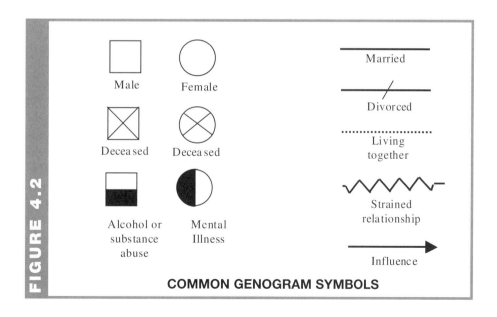

FIGURE 4.2

COMMON GENOGRAM SYMBOLS

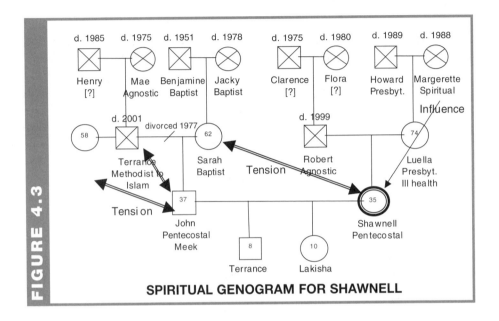

SPIRITUAL GENOGRAM FOR SHAWNELL

FIGURE 4.3

overwhelming and unexpected and may cause individuals to lose hope and faith. Alternatively, they can be enriching and transformative. The spirituality timeline can chart the important changes in—and trajectories of—clients' faith-journeys.

Figure 4.4 is Shawnell's spirituality timeline. Her faith slowly grew as an adolescent, when she attended a Presbyterian church with her mother. Shawnell had a conversion peak experience attending the Presbyterian church camp when she was 17. Thereafter she began dating, and her spirituality plateaued from age 18–21. Soon after she married, she became disillusioned with her husband, and her faith began to slip. Shawnell had a pit experience at age 25, when, shortly after having her first child, she was in a severe car accident. She was unable to understand "how God could have let such a thing happen." At age 28 she began attending a Pentecostal church, which resulted in an intensification in her faith life over the next three years. She experienced another such peak at that point when she experienced the "baptism in the Holy Spirit."

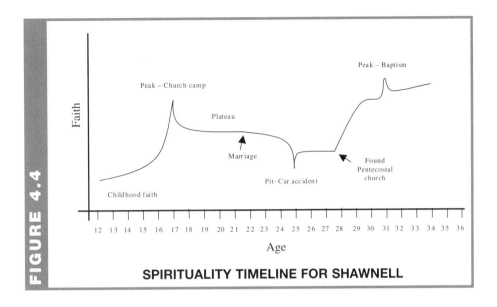

Faith

Peak – Baptism

Peak – Church camp

Plateau

Marriage

Childhood faith

Pit- Car accident

Found
Pentecostal
church

12　13　14　15　16　17　18　19　20　21　22　23　24　25　26　27　28　29　30　31　32　33　34　35　36

Age

SPIRITUALITY TIMELINE FOR SHAWNELL

FIGURE 4.4

Formal Instruments

Formal paper-and-pencil instruments provide another means of under-standing clients' religious and spiritual views. Such devices offer the additional benefit of assisting in differential diagnoses between religious/spiritual issues and those attributable to a mental disorder (Lukoff, Lu, & Turner, 1992; Stanard, Sandhu, & Painter, 2000). Formal spiritual assessments can be administered and scored quickly. They are helpful in diagnosis and treatment planning, and they provide springboards for therapeutic discussions. We will discuss three of the various assessment instruments available.

The Spiritual Assessment Inventory

The SAI (Hall & Edwards, 2002) is designed to measure individuals' awareness of God and the quality of their relationship with God. It contains five subscales: awareness, realistic acceptance, disappointment, grandiosity, and instability. There is a sixth additional experimental subscale called impression management. The SAI contains 47 items and uses a 5-point Likert scale ranging from 1, *not at all true,* to 5, *very true.* Examples of items include: "I seem to have a unique ability to influence God through my prayers," and "There are times when I feel disappointed with God." In one sample, the reliability alphas ranged from .73–.95 for the five subscales. Confirmatory factor analysis and sub-scale correlations with similar instruments suggest support for construct validity (Hall & Edwards).

The Index of Core Spiritual Experiences

The INSPIRIT (Kass, Friedman, Leserman, Zuttermeister, & Benson, 1991) is designed to assess the personal conviction that God exists and that God dwells within. The measure has 7 items, which fall into a single factor. Response options vary for each item. Examples of items include: "How often have you felt as though you were very close to a powerful spiritual force that seemed to lift you outside yourself?" and "Have you ever had an experience that has convinced you that God exists?" The original sample demonstrated a reliability alpha of .90, and comparisons with other measures suggest validity (Kass et al.).

The Spiritual Well-Being Scale

The SWBS (Ellison, 1983) assesses religious, existential, and spiritual well-being. It is the most researched spirituality measure to date (Stanard et al., 2000). It contains 20 items that provide existential well-being and religious well-being scores, as well as a composite spiritual well-being score. Ratings are completed using a 6-point Likert scale ranging from *strongly agree* to *strongly disagree.* An example item is "My relation with God contributes to my sense of well-being." Ellison reported reliability alphas from .78–.96 for the two sub-scales and composite score. Convergent and discriminant validity have been suggested by SWBS comparisons with measures of loneliness, self-esteem, life purpose, and intrinsic religious orientation (Ellison).

Summary

The FACE-SPIRIT model consists of implicit strategies—Focusing on the present, Asking for guidance, Compassion cultivation, and Existential empathy—and explicit strategies—Simile and metaphor, Prayer, Interpretation of sacred texts, Rituals, Imagery, and Transgression relief—for integrating spirituality into helping. It is vitally important to conduct religious and spiritual assessments with clients. The following five techniques assist in the spiritual assessment process: intake forms, clinical interviews, spiritual genograms, spirituality timelines, and formal paper-and-pencil instruments.

Discussion Questions and Activities

1. Given your particular religious and spiritual beliefs, would implicit or explicit strategies be more comfortable for you to implement in your counseling practice?

2. Which of the spiritual assessment strategies discussed in this chapter seem the most helpful to you? Can you think of specific clients or situations for which certain assessment techniques would be more useful than others? What are some examples?

3. Create a spiritual genogram for your own family. Can you identify patterns, themes, or relationships that are of particular interest? Are you able to gain insight from the genogram that helps to explain your current or past spiritual development?

4. Create a spirituality timeline for your life. What were the precipitous events that led to peaks and pits? Given your current spiritual development, would you now interpret some of the earlier events in your life differently? Where do you hope your spiritual timeline takes you in the coming 10 years?

PART

FACE – Implicit Strategies for Integrating Spirituality Into Counseling and Psychotherapy

*So the smart brain must be balanced with a warm heart,
a good heart—a sense of responsibility,
of concern for the well-being of others.*

– 14th Dalai Lama

In the first section of the book, we considered the *why, when,* and *how* of integrating spirituality into counseling and psychotherapy. Now it is time to turn our attention to the *FACE-SPIRIT* model itself and learn practical strategies for incorporating spirituality into our work with clients.

This section of the text will focus on implicit strategies that helping professionals can use to *indirectly* integrate spirituality into counseling and therapy—the *FACE* part of our model. The implicit strategies—*Focusing on the present, Asking for guidance, Compassion cultivation,* and *Existential empathy*—allow mental health professionals to infuse spirituality into therapy without directly engaging clients in the process. We believe that such strategies enable helping professionals to establish a core of openness and caring within themselves that will result in greater receptivity to clients and their needs.

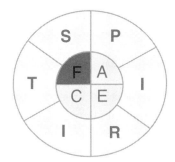

5

Focusing on the Present

What, at this moment, is lacking?

– Zen master Rinzai
(as cited in Tolle, 1999, p. 43)

If you answered the above question, you probably came up with the same answer as most people—"nothing." If nothing is lacking in the present moment, this leads to another question, "Why do we spend so much time either thinking about the past or future?" In this chapter, we will look at this tendency, its possible negative effects on the helping relationship, and potential solutions.

The Present Moment

If we were to look candidly at the percentage of time we are "in the present," we would probably find it to be rare. Due to the hectic pace of contemporary life, we tend to have a difficult time focusing on the present. We frequently think about the past with regret or dwell on the future with anxiety or wishful fantasies. Some argue that our minds are afraid to simply let go and embrace the present as it is (Foundation for Inner Peace, 1996; Tolle, 1999).

> End the delusion of time. Time and mind are inseparable. Remove time from the mind and it stops—unless you choose to use it. To be identified with your mind is to be trapped in time: the compulsion to live almost exclusively through memory and anticipation. This creates an endless preoccupation with past and future and an unwillingness to honor and acknowledge the present moment and *allow it to be.* The compulsion arises because the past gives you an identity and the future holds the promise of salvation, of fulfillment in whatever form. Both are illusions. (Tolle, p. 40)

The Buddha believed that one of the causes of pain and suffering is not being in the present moment (Selby, 2003). Twenty-five hundred years later, researchers have begun to corroborate Buddha's insights. In two studies, researchers found that individuals who had future rather than present time orientations had statistically significant higher rates of physical ailments, anxiety, and depressive symptoms (La Roche & Frankel, 1986). Our inability to stay in the present affects not only our physical and psychological well-being, but also our professional efficacy.

As therapists and human services workers, our responsibility is to attend to our clients. Numerous researchers have suggested the primary healing mechanism in psychotherapy is the therapeutic relationship (Wampold, 2001). However, we are often not as present for our clients as we need to be. We are frequently thinking about what we are going to say, whether we agree with our client's perspective, or how to interpret what was just said. We become mired in conceptualizing our client's case and debating possible interventions. And frankly we are also sometimes distracted by such thoughts as, "I'm hungry... I wonder how much time is left?" or "Is she going to discuss her Aunt Betty, *again*?" All these failures to be fully present to our clients can have a negative impact on the therapeutic relationship (see Box 5.1).

Focusing on the present makes the therapeutic relationship possible. Carl Rogers (1946, 1957) suggested the importance of being authentic and genuine as one of the core conditions for a healing relationship. He explained that in order for the change process to occur, we must be congruent, or in touch with our own feelings (Rogers, 1957).

When we are in the present moment, we cannot judge another person (Selby, 2003). Some consider that being nonjudgmental is essential in healing relationships (e.g., Enright & Fitzgibbons, 2000; Foundation for Inner Peace, 1992; Rogers, 1949, 1957).

Mindfulness is one way to speak about practicing the habit of focusing on the present. Mindfulness can be defined as focusing complete attention on the present moment with an attitude of nonjudgment and acceptance (Baer, Smith, Hopkins, Krietemeyer & Toney, 2006;

BOX 5.1

Focusing on the Present in Therapy

I (Charlie) recall one particular session when I was a doctoral student leading T-groups for master's counseling students. As any therapist knows, leading "group" can be challenging. There are numerous tasks that the leader must attend to, such as establishing norms, observing group processes, making process commentary, observing social dynamics, blocking, linking, and managing executive functioning tasks. One day I was deep in thought when I realized the group members were staring at me and waiting for a response. I had almost no idea what they had been discussing. I immediately turned bright red and managed to mumble something brilliant like, "Could someone repeat that last part again?" During supervision, I came to the conclusion that I had over 50% of my attention focused on my own thoughts rather than my group members' content. Big mistake.

When I'm training new therapists in basic counseling skills and they express difficulty integrating new techniques, I advise them, "Focus on the client. Worry less about what you are going to say." Invariably this helps. When they focus on the client, their new skills seem to emerge on their own.

Linehan, 1993a). In a study examining mindfulness, researchers found that individuals who were aware and nonjudgmental (i.e., who refrained from making evaluative labels) had significantly lower levels of anxiety and depression (Cashwell, Glosoff, & Hammond, 2007).

Mindfulness and Empirical Research

Mindfulness, or focusing on the present, is so effective that several counseling interventions have been developed based on this construct. Examples include mindfulness-based stress reduction (MBSR; Kabat-Zinn, 1982), acceptance and commitment therapy (ACT; Hayes, Strosahl, & Wilson, 1999), mindfulness-based cognitive therapy (MBCT; Segal, Williams, & Teasdale, 2002), and dialectical behavior therapy (DBT; Linehan, 1993a, 1993b).

In a meta-analysis examining 18 studies that used mindfulness training, Baer (2003) found generally positive results across the data. Patients suffering from chronic pain showed a statistically significant improvement in their pain scores and other psychological and medical symptoms. The researcher found significant improvements in groups with generalized anxiety and panic attacks, binge eating disorders, depression relapse prevention, fibromyalgia symptoms, and a mixed clinical sample (e.g., narcissistic and borderline personality disorders, anxiety, etc.). The overall mean effect size, based on the follow-up values in the individual studies, was .59 ($SD = .41$), which is considered a medium sized effect (Cohen, 1977). In a large study ($N = 1,350$) of Massachusetts prisoners who were taught MBSR, results indicated significant improvements across measures of hostility, self-esteem, and mood (Samuelson, Carmody, Kabat-Zinn, & Bratt, 2007). Analysis revealed that women inmates showed greater improvement than men, and those in minimum security prisons did better than their counterparts in higher security facilities.

Bishop (2003) conducted a meta-analysis of 13 MBSR studies, and was less positive than Baer (2003). Bishop's primary concern regarding the MBSR studies was a lack of control and methodological flaws. Although he believed there is currently a lack of evidence to recommend MBSR, he deemed there is sufficient support to warrant further investigation.

Methods of Focusing on the Present

Practices for focusing on the present originated more than 2,500 years ago and were systematically articulated in Buddhism (Kabat-Zinn, 2003). Although mindfulness practice is at the heart of Buddhist meditation (Kabat-Zinn; Thera, 1962) similar teachings occur in numerous other ancient traditions (e.g., Krishnamurti, 1991; Lao Tsu, 2003; Patanjali, 1982; Tolle, 1999). During the last 40 years mindfulness practices have taken hold in the West (Kabat-Zinn).

There are numerous methods for focusing on the present or experiencing mindfulness. They can be practiced informally during most daily activities as well as during specific sitting meditation or yoga sessions. The core of such practices is focused awareness on bodily sensations or breathing (Williams, Duggan, Crane, & Fennell, 2006) or observation of thoughts and emotions. The goal, however, is not to criticize or think about thoughts or feelings. It is to merely observe and release them on a moment-by-moment basis without evaluating or dwelling upon them. We will discuss some common methods of Focusing on the Present.

Focusing on Breathing

This may be the most common technique for Focusing on the Present. To experience this, sit comfortably in a chair with your feet on the floor. Close your eyes and pay attention to your breath as it flows in and out of your nostrils. Simply observe it moving in and out. Alternately, you may visualize "peace" flowing into you as you inhale, and "stress" or "frustration" flowing out of you as you exhale. Another alternative is to count while you inhale, hold your breath, exhale, and pause before inhaling again. Selby (2003) recommends inhaling for 4 counts, holding for 2, exhaling for 2, and holding for 2 counts. If you want greater alertness, try inhaling for 6 counts, holding for 4, exhaling for 2, and holding for 2 counts (Selby). The count for calming is inhaling for 2, holding for 2, exhaling for 6, and holding for 4 counts (Selby).

Focused Body Scan

People generally practice the focused body scan sitting or lying down. Pay attention to different parts of your body. You might try starting with your toes and slowly work your way up the body to end with the top of your head. What feelings or sensations do you notice in your body? Are there parts that are tired or sore? Are you hungry? A method similar to this can be seen in the vignette later in this chapter.

Observing Thoughts and Feelings

The technique of observing your thoughts and feelings constitutes an attempt to remove your Self (capital "S") from your ego mind and to become an outside observer of your thoughts. Sit quietly and notice your cognitions as they arise. Do not judge or criticize them but simply observe them. Notice any feelings or emotions that you may experience. Your goal is to avoid reacting to your thoughts and feelings and instead simply observe them.

Walking Meditation

In this practice, focus on your breath as you walk. Observe the air filling your lungs and diaphragm. Notice your body and breath as you exhale. You might try observing your body for other sensations. As an alternative, try coordinating your paces with each inhalation and exhalation (Selby, 2003). This process should help quiet the mind.

Mindful Eating

If you are eating alone, you can use this time to focus on the present. Notice the smells of the food. You can observe the visible colors and shapes. As you chew, focus on the taste, aroma, and texture of the food. Your goal is to engage fully in the sensory experience of eating.

Focusing on Two or More Points

Research suggests that the concentration required to observe two or more sensory data—for example, breathing and heartbeat—has a powerful effect on quieting the mind (Selby, 2003). This works not only with tactile sensations but also other senses. Try listening to ambient external sounds while paying attention to your breathing. Alternatively, you might focus on visual stimuli while noticing your breathing or your heartbeat.

You can apply these same principles to many other activities. If you practice Hatha yoga, try focusing on your breathing or bodily sensations while exercising. You can even focus on the present while brushing your teeth. Notice how the toothbrush handle feels in your hand. Experience the sensation of the bristles moving against your teeth and gums. Smell and taste the toothpaste. Most important, consider clearing and focusing your mind through the use of a centering technique before meeting with a client.

Vignette: Focusing on the Present Before Meeting With Shawnell

In this vignette, the counselor realizes he has only eight minutes before he needs to see his next client, Shawnell. He has just left a meeting with his boss during which they argued about salary inequities within the agency where he works. The counselor is shaken, anxious, and unprepared to meet with his client, so he decides to spend five minutes reviewing Shawnell's case notes to get his attention back on track. In the remaining three minutes, he focuses on his breathing and body as a way to make himself present, calm, and ready to meet his client.

He sits with both feet on the floor, closes his eyes, and focuses on his breathing, inhaling "peace" through his nose and exhaling "stress" through his mouth. He brings his attention to his diaphragm as he breathes, watching it rise and fall. He focuses on the feeling of his hands on the arm of the chair. He notices the weight of his body on his buttocks and thighs. When he finally turns his attention back to the task at hand, he feels ready to meet with Shawnell.

Summary

Staying in the present moment can be difficult, however, failing to do so can have a negative effect on both therapist well-being and the quality of the therapeutic relationship. Five techniques can assist mental health professionals in Focusing on the Present: focusing on breathing, a focused body scan, observing thoughts and feelings, walking meditation, and mindful eating. It can also be beneficial to focus on two or more objects.

Discussion Questions

1. How much of your time would you estimate that you are focused on the present moment? How much is spent in daydreaming or worrying about the past and future?
2. Why do you believe it is so difficult to stay in the present moment?
3. What techniques have you tried, if any, for focusing on the present? What seemed to work best for you? What failed to work, and why?
4. What new techniques for focusing on the present would you be willing to try?
5. During your daily routine (e.g., driving, preparing meals, taking a shower, etc.) when could you take time to practice using some of the suggested techniques to focus on the present?

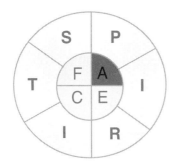

6

Asking for
Guidance

*Therapists who believe in God and think that God can
enlighten and guide people would be wise to regularly pray
for God's inspiration and guidance to assist them in
their work with clients.*

– Richards & Bergin (2005, p. 253)

The renowned therapist Irvin Yalom (1989) admitted that he strug-
gled to know what to do with his patients from one moment to the
next. All of us share this struggle in choosing interventions or
approaches in working with our clients. But must of us would agree
that we sometimes do our best work when we let go of our precon-
ceived notions of what course therapy should take during the session
and follow our intuitive leadings. While we can offer no conclusive
explanation of this experience, it is at least possible that we frame its
origin in terms of spirituality. Are we tapping into our unconscious
mind, a universal mind, collective consciousness, chi energy field, or a
higher power such as God or the Holy Spirit (Breslin & Lewis, 2008)?
Regardless of how we define this influence, it is clear that we need to
find ways of seeking it out and augmenting it. We are better therapists
when we request assistance from a higher power.

Reasons for Implicit Prayer
and Asking for Guidance

Privately praying for our client and asking for guidance prior to the session is an implicit strategy that is unencumbered by any ethical concerns (McCullough & Larson, 1999). In qualitative studies, secular counselors have offered many reasons why they pray to God or ask for guidance (Gubi, 2001, 2004). Some report that it helps them to ground themselves, quiet their minds, or balance themselves (Gubi, 2001, 2004). One respondent stated, "it is about becoming still so that I can focus on what I'm doing with the client" (Gubi, 2001, p. 428). They have described this practice as part of their preparation process. Others have explained it as helping them feel supported when they are overwhelmed, anxious, in a difficult situation, or uncertain about what to do (Gubi, 2001, 2004; Miller, 2003). It is also a way of diffusing resentment toward unlikable clients (McCullough & Larson).

Therapists report asking for God's guidance (see also Box 6.1) (Gubi, 2004), but not that God "control" the work of the therapist (p. 469). Others saw God's guidance as a supplement to their existing training, experience, and intuition. Some counselors noted that implicit prayer helps them feel that a higher power is "holding" their client (Gubi).

Frequency of Counselors Asking
for Guidance and Praying

How frequently do therapists pray for their clients? In a large national sample of social workers ($N = 1,167$), 57.9% of therapists reported having prayed for their clients in private (Canda & Furman, 1999). Of gerontologically oriented social workers in one sample ($N = 299$), 67% reported praying for their clients *sometimes* or *often* (Murdock as cited in Hodge, 2007). In a sample of secular British therapists ($N = 247$), 49% reported praying for their clients (Gubi, 2004). Over one half (51%) of the counselors used prayer to prepare themselves for their clients, 37% asked for guidance during the counseling session, and

BOX 6.1

A Spiritual Perspective on Guidance

This is an interesting selection from A Course in Miracles (Foundation for Inner Peace, 1976) about allowing God to guide a psychotherapy session. Depending on your spiritual views, you may find this distressing or comforting.

A therapist does not heal; he lets healing be. The Holy Spirit is the only Therapist. He makes healing clear in any situation in which He is the Guide. You can only let Him fulfill His function. He needs no help for this. He will tell you exactly what to do to help anyone He sends to you for help, and will speak to him through you if you do not interfere. Remember that you choose the guide for helping, and the wrong choice will not help. But remember also that the right one will. Trust Him, for help is His function, and He is of God. (p. 172–173)

59% used implicit prayer to enhance their work. In a group of mainstream British counselors ($N = 96$) who were referral sources for church clergy known as Church Ministerial Counselors, 65% reported asking for guidance during sessions and 54% had covertly prayed for their clients during the session (Gubi). Thus we may say that, in general, the majority of therapists privately pray for or ask for guidance for their clients.

Prayer and Measures of Well-Being

Research suggests that prayer improves one's well-being and that the act of praying itself may be therapeutic. In a study of religious variables and psychological well-being in a sample of undergraduate students in England ($N = 474$), researchers found that frequency of prayer had the strongest relationship with well-being (Maltby, Lewis, & Day, 1999). The participants who prayed more had lower rates of depression and anxiety and higher levels of self-esteem.

It may be noted that in a sample of female caregivers ($N = 155$) with children suffering from chronic illnesses, results indicated that educational level moderated the relationship between prayer and health symptoms and quality of life (Banthia, Moskowitz, Acree, & Folkman, 2007). Prayer was related with better health and quality of life for the less educated participants. This may be because the higher educated tend to have greater resources, so they are more likely to pray as a last resort or when they have hit rock bottom (Banthia et al.). In a study of family caregivers of dementia sufferers ($N = 1,229$), analyses revealed that frequency of prayer was associated with less depression in the caregivers (Hebert, Dang, & Schulz, 2007). However, frequency of prayer did not have a statistically significant relationship with complicated grief in the bereaved.

Types of Prayer

Prayer is often categorized into four types based on researchers' factor analysis (Poloma & Pendleton, 1989, 1991). The four types of prayer are colloquial, meditative, petitionary, and ritualistic. In this section, we will discuss each of these categories in detail. Examples of each appear in Table 6.1.

Colloquial Prayer

Colloquial prayer involves talking to God in one's own words. It may include thanking God for blessings, communicating love for God, asking for guidance in decision making, or asking God to forgive sins or end world suffering (Poloma & Pendleton, 1989, 1991). In one study, colloquial prayer was found to have a negative relationship with anxiety and depression (Maltby, Lewis, & Day, 2008). In another study, colloquial prayer was the only prayer type that was associated with happiness (Poloma & Pendleton, 1989). In a different sample, colloquial prayer was associated with happiness and religious satisfaction (Poloma & Pendleton, 1991).

TABLE 6.1	EXAMPLES BY THERAPIST AND CLIENT OF THE FOUR TYPES OF PRAYER		
	Type of Prayer	*Therapist Alone*	*Client Alone*
	Colloquial	"I am blessed to have such wonderful clients. Guide my sessions with them today."	"Please forgive my sins and help me live a righteous life."
	Meditative	Sitting in silence waiting for direction from a higher source	Sitting in silence, thinking about God, and feeling his/her presence
	Petitionary/ Intercessory	"Help my client through his depression and finding a job."	"Help me find a job."
	Ritualistic	Reciting the prayer of St. Francis of Assisi	Stating the Christian Lord's Prayer

Source: Adapted from "Exploring types of prayer and quality of life: A research note," by M. M. Poloma and B. F. Pendleton, 1989, *Review of Religious Research, 31,* pp. 46–53, and "The effects of prayer and prayer experiences on measures of general well-being," by M. M. Poloma and B. F. Pendleton, 1991, *Journal of Psychology and Theology, 19,* p. 71–83.

Meditative Prayer

Meditative prayer is the only nonverbal type of prayer. It consists of activities such as sitting in God's presence, thinking about God, adoring God, and listening for God's personal address (Poloma & Pendleton, 1989, 1991). Meditative prayer is associated with life satisfaction, existential well-being, happiness, and religious satisfaction (Poloma & Pendleton, 1989, 1991). It has been shown to have an inverse relationship with anxiety, depression, social dysfunction, and somatic symptoms (Maltby et al., 2008).

Petitionary Prayer

Petitionary prayer involves making specific requests to God for material things for oneself or another (Kelly, 1995; Poloma & Pendleton, 1991). If the request is for another individual, it is commonly referred to as intercessory prayer (Hodge, 2007). When the prayer is for oneself, it is often motivated by the need to reduce frustration and make adjustments to one's life (Poloma & Pendleton, 1991). In two different samples, petitionary prayer had a nonstatistically significant relationship with measures of well-being (Maltby et al., 2008; Poloma & Pendleton, 1989). In a third study, however, petitionary prayer was associated with negative affect and religious satisfaction (Poloma & Pendleton, 1991). We will discuss research findings of intercessory prayer in detail in chapter 10.

Ritualistic Prayer

Ritualistic prayer is the act of reciting a prayer from a book or from memory (Poloma & Pendleton, 1989, 1991). In one sample, ritualistic prayer was the only one of the four to be associated with negative affect (Poloma & Pendleton, 1989). This result was also found in another sample, where it was related with religious satisfaction (Poloma & Pendleton, 1991). Others have suggested that those who use ritualistic prayer are more likely to be sad, lonely, and tense (Richards & Bergin, 2005). However, another study has suggested that ritualistic prayer has an inverse relationship with depression, anxiety, social dysfunction, and somatic complaints in a sample of British adults (Maltby et al., 2008).

Examples of Asking for Guidance

If one chooses to ask for guidance from a higher power, it is fitting to use a method compatible with one's beliefs and values. Below we have listed several forms of asking for guidance. The first is from *A Course in Miracles* (Foundation for Inner Peace, 1976).

> I am here only to be truly helpful. I am here to represent
> Him who sent me. I do not have to worry about what to say

or what to do, because He who sent me will direct me.
I am content to be wherever He wishes, knowing He goes
there with me. I will be healed as I let Him teach me to heal.
(p. 28)

It has been suggested that Saint Francis of Assisi be regarded as the patron saint of counselors. The famous prayer attributed to him is an excellent model for counselors to use to ask for guidance. It is particularly powerful in helping to develop empathy (Garrett, 1994).

The Prayer of St. Francis

Lord, make me an instrument of your peace.
Where there is hatred, let me sow love;
where there is injury, pardon;
where there is doubt, faith;
where there is despair, hope;
where there is darkness, light;
and where there is sadness, joy.

O Divine Master, grant that I may not so much seek
to be consoled as to console;
to be understood as to understand;
to be loved as to love.
For it is in giving that we receive;
it is in pardoning that we are pardoned;
and it is in dying that we are born to eternal life. Amen

Some argue that seeking divine guidance is as natural as "breathing air" (Foundation for Inner Peace, 1976, p. 280). "You taught yourself the most unnatural habit of not communicating with your Creator. Unlearn isolation through His loving guidance, and learn of all the happy communication that you have thrown away but could not lose" (p. 278). We hope that if you seek guidance before or during your sessions with clients that you find what you seek and that the experience is helpful and healing.

Vignette

The counselor desires to feel more grounded before he meets Shawnell. He also hopes to feel inspired and perhaps guided by a higher power as he works with her. He chooses to ask for guidance in a format that he uses at his local Unity church:

> Father, Mother, God, I know that the divine intelligence of the universe is everywhere and in everything. It surrounds me and fills me. And I know that I am part of the one mind, so my thoughts and words are coming from the divine. I know that your spirit will guide me when I work with Shawnell in a few moments. I know I will accurately hear and perceive her situation, conceptualize her issues, and have divine inspiration when formulating interventions with her. I am thankful for this guidance knowing it is for Shawnell's highest good. I release these words, and I give thanks for this and know it is so … and so it is. Amen.

Summary

Asking for guidance from a higher power before or during a session is reported to help therapists quiet their minds and balance themselves. Research suggests that a majority of helping professionals practice this strategy before seeing their clients. We discussed four types of prayer—colloquial, meditative, petitionary, and ritualistic—and provided several examples of ritualistic prayers.

Discussion Questions

1. Do you pray or ask for guidance from a higher source?
2. If so, what benefits do you receive, if any?
3. Do you (or would you) pray for your clients outside of therapy sessions?
4. If you pray for clients, how do you choose which clients you are going to pray for?

7

Compassion Cultivation

Compassion is not religious business, it is human business,
it is not luxury, it is essential for our own peace and
mental stability, it is essential for human survival.

– 14th Dalai Lama

After asking for guidance, the next part of our model is the "C" in FACE, which stands for Compassion Cultivation. The cultivation of compassion may be considered to be the very foundation of counseling and helping, because compassion—closely linked to universal love—allows us to have unconditional positive regard for our clients and ourselves. It puts the heart in what we do.

According to Viktor Frankl (1984), the founder of existential therapy:

> Love is the only way to grasp another human being in the innermost core of his personality. No one can become fully aware of the very essence of another human being unless he loves him. By his love he is enabled to see the essential traits and features in the beloved person; and even more, he sees that which is potential in him, which is not yet actualized but

yet ought to be actualized. Furthermore, by his love, the loving person enables the beloved person to actualize these potentialities. By making him aware of what he can be and of what he should become, he makes these potentialities come true. (p. 134)

The concept of compassion—an outpouring of loving-kindness can be found to have roots in all major wisdom traditions. In Judaism, the liturgy portrays God as a bestower of loving-kindness who remembers the good deeds of the patriarchs and lovingly brings a redeemer to their descendents (Wieder as cited in Ramon, 2005). As God bestows loving-kindness or steadfast love (*hesed*) on His people, so the people are to bestow it on others as an essential human grace.

In the Christian tradition, compassion for others is expressed in its highest form through *agape* (or love), which is said by St. Paul to be the greatest of all spiritual gifts (1 Cor. 13). Agape, as described by Vacek (1994), focuses on the beloved's value and seeks to enhance that value. It is faithful, spontaneous, generous, and self-sacrificial. Isaac of Ninevah was an eighth century Christian monk whose discourse on love illuminates the character of agape in a striking manner:

What is the sum of purity? A heart full of mercy unto the whole created nature .... And what is a merciful heart? ... The burning of the heart unto the whole creation, man, fowls and beasts, demons and whatever exists, so that by the recollection and the sight of them the eyes shed tears on account of the force of mercy which moves the heart by great compassion. Then the heart becomes weak [small] and it is not able to bear hearing or examining injury or any insignificant suffering of anything in the creation. And therefore even in behalf of the irrational beings and the enemies of truth and even in behalf of those who do harm to it, at all times he offers prayers with tears that they may be guarded and strengthened; even in behalf of the kinds of reptiles, on account of his great compassion which is poured out in his heart without measure, after the example of God. (Isaac as cited in Oord, 2007, p. 128)

Templeton (1999) contends that agape is an underlying principle in all major world religions and that everyone on earth has the option to grow in it. Agape, which is said to be an expression of God's love radiating through us, can be thought of as an invitation to true happiness for ourselves and others.

Similarly, within the Islamic tradition, compassion can be assumed to be much like the selfless love described by a Sufi mystic, Muhaiyaddeen (1981), who stated,

> We must draw that grace and that treasure within us. This love is true love, the love borne of faith and trust, the love borne of brotherly unity, the love that comes from being one family, the love that comes from prayer, the love that comes from merging with God, the love which has no limit. (p. 20)

This selfless love allows one to have deep empathy for the suffering of others, as Muhaiyaddeen went on to say, "Once you have God's love, God's qualities, and God's actions, everyone is connected to you, and therefore you will feel the suffering no matter whose it is" (p. 24).

Compassion is also closely linked to *metta,* the Buddhist practice of loving-kindness. *Metta,* derived from the Pali word, *mitta,* has been translated as "a true friend in need," and was used by the Buddha to promote friendliness and to eliminate ill will (Ñanomoli, 1987). The immense merit associated with *metta* was explained by the Buddha in the Itivuttaka, Suta 27:

> Just as whatever light there is of stars, all is not worth one sixteenth part of the moon's; in shining and beaming and radiance the moon's light far excels it; and just as in the last month of the Rains, in the Autumn when the heavens are clear, the sun as it climbs the heavens drives all darkness from the sky with its shining and beaming and radiance; and just as, when night is turning to dawn, the morning star is shining and beaming and radiating; so too, whatever kinds of worldly merit there are, all are not worth one sixteenth part of the heart-deliverance of loving-kindness; in shining and beaming and radiance the heart-deliverance of loving-kindness far excels them. (Ñanomoli, 1987)

Loving-kindness is multifaceted and involves developing an all-embracing kindness (affective dimension), desiring to make others happy rather than causing hatred or suffering (cognitive dimension), and generating only friendliness among all living beings (behavioral dimension). In Thailand, compassion and loving-kindness, which are usually studied together, have been found to be the most important variables in nursing care and to have the greatest benefits for patients (Jormsri, Kunaviktikul, Ketefian, & Chaowalit, 2005).

Compassion and loving-kindness also produce positive results for the person doing the practice. Experimental studies with patients at Duke University Medical Center found loving-kindness meditation brought relief from persistent back pain, psychological distress, and anger (Archer, 2005). In addition, studies suggest that self-compassion, or compassion extended toward oneself, attenuates individuals' reactions to negative events in ways that are different from and, in some cases, more beneficial than self-esteem (Leary, Tate, Allen, Adams, & Hancock, 2007).

Because of the enormous benefits of cultivating compassion toward oneself and others, we have included *Compassion Cultivation* as the *C* in the *FACE-SPIRIT* model. Before seeing clients, we like to cultivate compassion by doing a short visualization, derived from the Buddhist practice of loving-kindness meditation. Kornfield (1993, 2005) and others suggest that this practice should begin by first extending loving-kindness to yourself, because without being at peace with yourself, it is probably impossible to help anyone else. Visualize yourself as being a beloved child and being well, happy, and peaceful.

Next, visualize someone in your life who is deeply respected and from whom you have received much care, love, and support. This individual should be someone toward whom you can easily extend loving thoughts and compassion. You would then extend loving-kindness to that person.

Loving-kindness would then be extended outward to others, such as to friends, acquaintances, and the client. If you wish, loving-kindness may be extended out still farther to people everywhere, and to all living beings. You can eventually extend this compassion to your enemies and to the most difficult people in your life. The key to this practice, however, is that you *feel* the compassion, rather than mentally verbalizing empty words.

In the following vignette, we'll share how one therapist cultivates compassion before seeing her clients. This simple method of doing the practice of loving-kindness consists of silently articulating the following affirmations, while visualizing the individuals surrounded by love.

Vignette

> May I be well, happy, and peaceful. May I also have patience, courage, and wisdom.
>
> May my family be well, happy, and peaceful. May they also have patience, courage, and wisdom.
>
> May my friends be well, happy, and peaceful. May they also have patience, courage, and wisdom.
>
> May my client (name) be well, happy, and peaceful. May he (or she) also have patience, courage, and wisdom.
>
> May all neutral people be well, happy, and peaceful. May they also have patience, courage, and wisdom.
>
> May my enemies be well, happy, and peaceful. May they also have patience, courage, and wisdom.
>
> May all beings everywhere be well, happy, and peaceful. May they also have patience, courage, and wisdom.

Research suggests that loving-kindness meditation can be a particularly powerful means to actively cultivate universal capacities for love, connectedness, and compassion (Kristeller & Johnson, 2005). Contemplative prayer practices from Christianity and other wisdom traditions, however, are likely to have similar effects and can also be used to cultivate compassion. Therefore feel free to choose a method of compassion cultivation that is comfortable for you, and try doing it before your sessions. We have found this practice allows us to have greater sensitivity to our clients' suffering and thus gives us the capacity for heightened empathy, which will be the topic of our next chapter.

Summary

Compassion, which has roots in most major wisdom traditions, is considered by some to be the very foundation of helping. Compassion Cultivation, represented by the *C* in *FACE-SPIRIT,* can be developed through the practice of loving-kindness meditation or similar contemplations to enhance helpers' ability to be receptive and caring toward their clients.

Discussion Questions

1. In your opinion, could a helping professional who lacked compassion ever be truly effective? Why or why not?
2. When do you think cultivating compassion might be especially important?
3. What practices have you used to cultivate compassion toward yourself and others?
4. What specific outcomes have you experienced as a result of such practices?

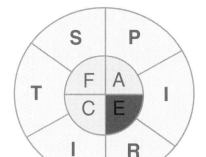

Existential Empathy

"If you just learn a single trick, Scout,
you'll get along a lot better with all kinds of folks.
You never really understand a person until
you consider things from his point of view …
until you climb inside of his skin and walk around in it."

– To Kill a Mockingbird

The last implicit component of the model—the *E* in *FACE*—stands for *Existential Empathy*. Existential Empathy consists of listening for the spiritual yearning of the client, the deeper longing behind the words, the *logos* or meaning that the client is striving to find in his or her life. Similar to Frankl's logotherapy, Existential Empathy involves more than simply hearing the ordinary details that are conveyed through the client's stories. Instead it consists of attending to the client's engagement with the larger issues that are inherent in existence itself. According to Frankl (1984), "this striving to find a meaning in one's life is the primary motivational force in man" (p. 121), and we believe that through Existential Empathy we can assist clients in this quest.

The I/Thou Relationship

How then do we achieve Existential Empathy? The answer begins and ends with the relationship that we have with our clients. The great existential theologian, Martin Buber (1970), assumed that, as humans, we live in a state of betweenness; that is there is never just an *I* but always an *other*. If we are fully present in the moment and honor the personhood of the other individual, an *I/Thou* relationship exists; but if we relate to the other person as a mere object, then an *I/It* relationship prevails. Buber emphasized the importance of *presence*, which serves three functions in human relationships: (1) it enables true I/Thou relationships to occur, (2) it allows for meaning to exist in a situation, and (3) it enables an individual to be responsible in the here-and-now (Gould as cited in Corey, 2005, p. 133).

In the I/Thou encounter, true transcendence can occur, and Existential Empathy becomes possible. Building upon Buber's thought, the noteworthy Jewish philosopher, Immanuel Levinas (1985) described how we are unconditionally called to respond to alterity, or the "otherness of the other" through our encountering "the face": "The Other, in the rectitude of his face, is not a character within a context ... the face is meaning all by itself" (p. 86). The face transcends any and all comprehension; it is "uncontainable and leads you beyond" (p. 87). Through the face-to-face encounter with the other person and the call to enact moral justice that it entails, Levinas claims that we are propelled beyond ourselves and have a glimpse of ultimate reality:

> There can be no 'knowledge' of God separated from the relationship with men. The Other is the very locus of metaphysical truth, and is indispensable for my relation with God. (p. 78)

If we can be fully present in an I/Thou relationship with our client, the most profound issues of existence can emerge and be explored. Existential themes that often surface in therapy include death, freedom, anxiety, isolation, and meaninglessness. Frankl taught that persons achieve authentic self-transcendence and experience wholeness only by facing and finding meaning in suffering (May, 1989; Frankl, 1984).

Existential Empathy

When helping professionals provide Existential Empathy, clients get in touch with their real selves and make deliberate choices consonant with who they really are. Clients can then decide what is truly best for them, rather than merely striving to live up to the expectations of others. According to Frankl (1984), "The logotherapist's role consists of widening and broadening the visual field of the patient so that the whole spectrum of potential meaning becomes conscious and visible to him" (pp. 132–133). This meaning must be discovered by the individual himself or herself, however, as it cannot be given by sources outside the self (Frankl). We believe that Existential Empathy entails being in relation with, and honoring, your client as though you were two travelers, embarking together on a sacred journey.

On this journey of discovery, each pebble along the path has significance, but its true worth is only revealed when the proper attention and reverence is shown. Full consciousness is required, as well as a belief that every detail has meaning and is to be valued, while together you encounter each phase of the winding course. Every bend along this trail offers clues as to the ultimate meaning and purpose of the client's life, but only with total attention may these clues be found. But how do we achieve this state of attention?

Simone Weil (1973) considered attention to be different from thought and concerned with a different level of consciousness:

> Attention consists of suspending our thought, leaving it detached, empty and ready to be penetrated by the object, it means holding our minds, within reach of this thought, but on a lower level and not in contact with it. (p. 72)

We suggest using the first three implicit strategies of our model (Focusing on the Present, Asking for Guidance, and Compassion

Cultivation) to quiet our minds and achieve the openness and receptivity to our client necessary for Existential Empathy to occur. With a still mind, listen for existential themes and be aware of deeper issues that may lie below the surface concerns of daily living. Allow the unity that arises from your face-to-face encounter with your client to take you beyond separateness and to reach a level where genuine meaning can be found.

In the words of an Indian guru, Gangaji (1995), be vigilant in paying attention:

> Vigilance is attention. Attention gets its attentiveness from pure awareness which you are. Self-definition only keeps you fixated on waves while yearning for the deep. The ocean has no problems with waves. Never for a moment does the ocean imagine the waves as separate from itself. Never for a moment does the ocean imagine there is any separation between wave and depth.
>
> Be the ocean. This is vigilance. (p. 156)

Vignette

With such vigilance and respect, we believe that Existential Empathy is possible. In the following passage, you will see a transcript of the therapist using Existential Empathy in working with our client, Dale. Note how the therapist helps Dale move beyond the more mundane issues to his real concerns.

Dale: Money is no longer an issue because of my inheritance, so what now? Steve was suggesting that I go back to school and take some graduate courses. I don't know. I guess I could. But I don't know what I'd want to study. I suppose I could do something that I really enjoyed or that mattered to someone, but what would that be? I don't even know what I enjoy anymore, much less what matters ... sometimes it seems pointless to do anything at all.

Therapist: (Silently nodding). *As I listen to Dale, I realize that his real issue might involve the need to feel that he's making a contribution, that he has something of value to give to his relationships and to the world. Dale's longing to do something that matters—and his own questioning of who he really is—will guide my response.*

Therapist: You seem to feel lost and unsure of what you have to offer to the world and to yourself. Maybe there's even some uncertainty about who you really are, and that immobilizes you.

Dale: That's it exactly. I do wonder who I am, now that I'm not an accountant anymore. I didn't really respect myself much in that role, but at least I had a sense of who I was, even though that person wasn't someone I ever wanted to be. (Pausing). Sometimes I feel guilty too. Why should I have so much when others have so little? I didn't do anything to deserve it.

Therapist: I hear you asking how your situation fits into some higher plan. You really wish you could make sense of it all and not feel so empty and maybe unworthy. You just want to understand your place in the universe and be at peace.

Dale: Yes, I want to feel that I'm practicing the right livelihood and that my life has meaning beyond just enjoying myself with material things.

Therapist: So what do you suppose might constitute the right livelihood?

Dale: Ah, that *is* the question! And that's something I've never really considered in much depth before now.

As you observed in this example, Existential Empathy helped to get to the heart of Dale's issue. The therapist offered Dale freedom, within a safe and supportive context, to explore what truly might give meaning to his life. Within the security of their trusting relationship, Dale was able to face the underlying concerns that would ultimately need to be addressed to find fulfillment and lasting happiness.

There are times, however, when we may wish to use not only implicit but also explicit strategies in counseling, which brings us to the end of FACE and the beginning of SPIRIT in our model. In the next section of the book, we will begin to examine strategies for directly incorporating spirituality into counseling and psychotherapy.

Summary

Existential Empathy involves a special type of listening in which helping professionals seek to understand and assist clients in their quest for meaning. By providing Existential Empathy, counselors and therapists help clients address ultimate concerns and achieve a deeper degree of understanding. As they face the suffering inherent in existence, clients will be empowered to move beyond surface concerns to achieve a more meaningful and fulfilling existence. Existential Empathy can only be accomplished when the helping professional maintains full awareness and deep respect for each moment shared with the client in his or her therapeutic journey toward truth.

Discussion Questions

1. What existential themes have you encountered in your own life? What impact have they had on you?
2. What do you think about the existentialist idea that finding meaning in suffering is the key to authentic self-transcendence? Why might this be true?
3. What do you consider to be at the core of most human suffering? Explain.
4. What does "sharing a sacred journey with your client" mean to you?
5. How might you personally achieve the state of awareness necessary for Existential Empathy to be present?

SPIRIT – Explicit Strategies for Integrating Spirituality Into Counseling and Psychotherapy

If I have been of service, if I have glimpsed more of the nature and essence of ultimate good, if I am inspired to reach wider horizons of thought and action, if I am at peace with myself, it has been a successful day.

– Alex Noble

In the last section of the book, we explored implicit strategies that helping professionals can use to *indirectly* integrate spirituality into counseling and therapy—the FACE part of our model. In this section, we'll focus on the second half of the model—SPIRIT—the explicit strategies that can be utilized to *directly* incorporate spirituality into our work with clients. Before discussing the SPIRIT interventions, however, we must emphasize the critically important caveat that these interventions should never be pushed on clients. To attempt to do so would be to meet the needs of the counselor rather than the client. Explicit strategies should be used only if clients ask for them or if the counselor knows they are appropriate. Even if the therapist is fairly certain that the interventions would be acceptable to the client, it is helpful to ask the client's permission before attempting to use them.

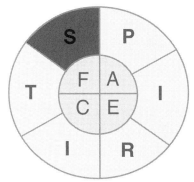

Simile and Metaphor

*Figured and metaphorical expressions do well to
illustrate more abstruse and unfamiliar ideas,
which the mind is not yet thoroughly accustomed to.*

– John Locke

The *S* in SPIRIT refers to the use of Simile and Metaphor, which can be employed to help clients work through concerns that they may find difficult to express. Similes and metaphors compare two seemingly dissimilar objects, such as "My heart is like the ocean," or "I am a rock." Similes and metaphors can be used to convey feelings and work through issues that are hard to verbalize. Additionally, they are useful in problem solving. Gladding (1989) said that similes and metaphors work because they help us see our lives in new ways by making the strange familiar and the familiar strange. Using similes and metaphors can increase clients' feelings of competence and connectedness, and may be useful for reframing the way they view their problems. In marriage counseling, metaphor has been used to give couples' problems definition and boundary. For example, when a therapist compared one couple's unresolved family-of-origin issues to a two-headed dragon living under their bed, the two marital partners decided to join forces to slay *it,* rather than each other (Grosch, 1988).

The Unique Power of Simile and Metaphor

We believe similes and metaphors are especially efficacious in helping clients get in touch with existential issues and ultimate concerns because they point beyond the mundane nature of everyday reality and allow us to connect with truths that are otherwise ineffable. This characteristic of symbolism is made evident in Gadamer's (1986) explanation of the meaning of the term *symbol*:

> Originally it was a technical term in Greek for a token of remembrance. The host presented his guest with the so-called *tessera hospitalis* by breaking some object in two. He kept one half for himself and gave the other half to his guest. If in thirty or fifty years' time, a descendant of the guest should ever enter his house, the two pieces could be fitted together again to form a whole in an act of recognition. In its original technical sense, the symbol represented something like a sort of pass used in the ancient world: something in and through which we recognize someone already known to us. (p. 31)

The symbolic power of similes and metaphors is immense because they help to connect us to existential and spiritual realities that we may know on a very deep level but find difficult to articulate in ordinary language. The choice to pause and take time to explore simile and metaphor is a deliberate and profound one, as Whitman suggested when he said that in order to write poetry, one "must loaf and invite [his] soul." For, as Gadamer illustrates, the symbols found in similes and metaphors allow us to recognize and connect with that which heals. They thus offer us a valuable means of broaching and addressing spiritual concerns in counseling and psychotherapy. Witmer (as cited in Wubbolding, 1993) asserts that similes and metaphors serve three pur poses: "to give us greater understanding of what is already known, to provide us with greater insight into the unknown, and to enable us to express that which has aesthetic and emotional intensity" (p. 22).

The use of simile and metaphor is part of a long and hallowed tradition that has been an essential educational and psychotherapeutic tool in many cultures throughout history, the practice of storytelling. One of the best known practitioners of this tradition was Jesus, who used parables to communicate life-changing truth. According to Close (1984), "These stories (parables, metaphors, allegories) have a power to communicate what logic and reason cannot duplicate. Part of the reason for this may be that logic has a way of *demanding* that you accept its truth, that you make it your own. A parable merely *invites* you to embrace its truth, and is thus much less likely to stir up resistance and defensiveness" (p. 298). Close's scientific rationale for this difference is based upon research showing that logic and metaphor operate in different hemispheres of the brain. While the left brain is rational, digital, and governs functions such as language, logic, and math, the right brain is intuitive, analogical, and is the seat of functions such as feelings, art, music, and one's basic worldview. If psychopathology is thought of as a disturbed worldview, then therapy should address the right hemisphere, where one's worldview resides. Logic speaks more to the left hemisphere (i.e., the conscious mind), while simile and metaphor speak to the right brain (i.e., the unconscious mind), thus granting stories tremendous power to bring about changes in one's outlook on life. Thus similes and metaphors can serve as invaluable tools in therapy to help clients work with their deepest, most inaccessible concerns.

Integrating Simile and Metaphor Into Counseling

Spontaneous Integration

In counseling and therapy, similes and metaphors are sometimes mentioned spontaneously by the client. When this occurs, it is important for helping professionals to listen carefully and follow the client's lead in exploring them. For example, if the client states that asking her husband to change is likely "to bring down the wrath of God," the therapist might ask her to describe the qualities of this wrathful God and how they might relate to her husband. In further discussion, she may reveal that she sees her husband as a punitive God who demands compliance to his wishes, while her wifely duty is to obey rather than request that he change. In other cases, the therapist might take the initiative and ask the client to think of a simile or metaphor to represent existential issues.

Homework Assignments

On a more concrete level, we like to assign the between-session task of asking clients to find and bring in a tangible object that represents spirituality to them or that illustrates the role that spirituality plays in their lives. Because having a tangible object to hold often makes it easier to talk about the highly personal and elusive issues inherent in spirituality, we have found this method to be particularly useful. The object can be anything that is meaningful to the client, although we have found abstract symbols to be more beneficial than items with preexisting meaning (e.g., crucifixes or stars of David). As an example of an abstract symbol, one client wondered if he had done the assignment correctly when he brought in a clothespin as a simile for his spirituality. We affirmed that the clothespin was totally appropriate when he disclosed that it was primarily his faith that held his life together. As homework, clients might also be asked to write a poem to describe a concern or issue that troubles them.

Integration With Sacred Text

Another way to employ simile and metaphor in psychotherapy is to ask clients if they can think of any character or situation in a holy book, such as the Bible or Koran, that could symbolically represent events or situations in their own lives. For example, a parolee who had been convicted of petty larceny recalled that his time in prison had been like that of Jonah in the belly of the whale. This ex-convict believed that his criminal acts had resulted from his turning from God, and so he used his time in incarceration to get back on track.

Reframing

Sometimes similes can be used to help clients reframe the way they think about what they are experiencing in order to gain strength or feel empowered. For example, if a client states, "Dealing with my situation is going to be like slaying Goliath," the therapist might stay with the client's simile and ask, "So how might David deal with your problem?" In other cases, the helping professional might ask, "What would Jesus do?" or "What would the Buddha say about that?" depending, of course, on the client's spiritual tradition.

Vignette

In the following transcript, the therapist uses simile and metaphor to help Dale get in touch with some of his deeper concerns. In the previous session, Dale was assigned the homework task of finding an object that could represent the role that spirituality played in his life to bring to his next meeting with his counselor.

Therapist: Hi, Dale. How are you today?

Dale: I'm fine, and I did my homework!

Therapist: You seem very pleased! I commend you for taking the assignment seriously. So what did you bring?

Dale: Well, I have this miniature rose blossom. I think I'd have to say that spirituality to me is like this tiny flower that gives great beauty to my life but is very fragile and easily crushed.

Therapist: So it sounds like you deeply value the role that spirituality plays in your existence, but you regret that it's sometimes so delicate and tenuous.

Dale: Yeah, I feel like it just gets pulled up by the roots or stomped on too often.

Therapist: Can you tell me more about how that happens?

Dale: Well, I've always been kind of mystical, and when I was a kid, I used to try to talk to my mother about some of my transcendent experiences. Like one day, I told her that I felt like if I looked up into the evening sky and stared at a star long enough, that I could fly up and go there. She told me to stop talking crazy or she would send me to a psychiatrist. Her words had such an impact on me that I not only stopped telling her about what I felt—I also stopped looking up at the night sky.

Therapist: So your mom stomped on your flower.

Dale: Yes, she did, and from that day on, I've questioned the legitimacy of my spiritual inclinations. Yet at the same time, they exist. I would even say that they are the parts of my life that seem most real and beautiful. Without them, I feel as dead as a crushed flower, yet the flower continues to be destroyed by people who don't even realize what they're doing.

Therapist: Maybe we should talk about ways that you can protect the flower ... that's so beautiful, but so fragile.

Dale: Yeah, I think I need to build a wall around it with a moat, so no one can ever hurt it again.

Therapist: I wonder how that might relate to your relationship with Steve.

Dale: Probably a lot. I know that I do that. I shut him out, along with everyone else, even though he's never done anything to hurt me.

Therapist: Maybe you should think about having a bridge and a gate to go along with your wall and moat. That way you could still protect the precious flower, but the ones you trust could come in and water it.

Dale: Yes, that would be great. I like that image!

As you can see, the flower simile—along with those of the castle, moat, and bridge—were very powerful for Dale. But what might have happened if Dale had forgotten his assignment or been reluctant to bring in an object? Having a Simile Box in the therapist's office can come in quite handy at such times. Included in a Simile Box may be small items, such as a sun and a moon, shells, feathers, stones, silk flowers, animals, hearts, and other things that can serve as similes.

Clients can be asked to select one item from the Simile Box that represents their own spiritual path or development and then consider questions such as: "How might this object be a simile or metaphor for your spiritual development?" "How might it reflect the function of spiritualty in your life?" and "What might be a symbol for the place you would like it to have in the future?" For example, a young male client selected a tiny pebble to represent the role that spirituality played in his life now, saying that it was his foundation, but that he hoped it would become a big boulder in the future.

Even without any tangible symbolic aids, however, similes and metaphors are easy to use, with clients being asked to simply verbally express their similes and metaphors. As long as clients can think abstractly, the latter method typically works quite well. We have observed that even when clients mention simple metaphors in jest, profound discussions often result. Consider the case of the woman who jokingly stated, "My spirituality is like this dried up leaf. It's not green and vibrant and supple anymore." Remembering what it was like to experience new growth and the first dew of spring, she longed for the sense of connection she had felt in an earlier season of her life when the leaf was still attached to the tree. In the ensuing exploration of what it was like to have fallen from the tree, her sense of isolation and disconnection from life-giving sources became apparent. The power of symbols is not to be underestimated.

Summary

Similes and metaphors promote seeing the world differently and can be used to help clients express feelings that are difficult to express. By serving as symbols for the ineffable, similes and metaphors offer pathways for clients to delve into the domain of ultimate concerns and to be healed and empowered.

Discussion Questions

1. What would be a simile or metaphor for the role that spirituality plays in your life? Why?
2. Can you think of some specific similes or metaphors that might be useful to clients who are in need of healing?
3. What are some examples of self-defeating similes or metaphors that clients might hold? How could these be reframed into more productive ones?
4. As you consider the various wisdom traditions, what scriptural characters or events might serve as symbols to help clients who are trying to make changes in their lives? How might you use these references to inspire or empower clients?
5. Find an object that can represent your view of spirituality. What characteristics of this object symbolize spirituality for you? Would you expect to choose the same object in the future or a different one? Why?

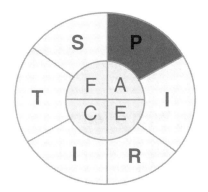

CHAPTER 1

Prayer

*Prayer is as natural an expression of faith
as breathing is of life*

– Jonathan Edwards (1703–1758)

The role of prayer in secular counseling is controversial (Basham & O'Connor, 2005; Frame, 2003; Gubi, 2001; Hodge, 2007; Kelly, 1995; Koenig & Pritchett, 1998; Wade, Worthington, & Vogel, 2007). Of the 10 spiritual strategies suggested in this model, it is the most contested. We have seen it give rise to heated debates among therapists. This concern originates, in part, from the potential ethical issues it raises, and it is therefore considered inappropriate by many therapists (Carlson, Kirkpatrick, Hecker, & Killmer, 2002; Richards & Bergin, 2005; Weld & Eriksen, 2007). Although there are some who would argue that prayer should never occur in therapy, there are many who believe that it is appropriate under the correct conditions (e.g., Basham & O'Connor; Frame; Weld & Eriksen). In fact, some contend that it may be unethical *not* to pray with devout clients in situations where it seems appropriate (Richards & Bergin; Richards & Potts, 1995; Weld & Eriksen).

Frequency of Counselors Praying With Clients

The percentage of therapists who pray or have prayed with their clients appears to vary according to the type of therapist (e.g., psychologist, social worker, etc.) and the setting. Christian counselors utilize prayer frequently, and it is their primary spiritual intervention (Ball & Goodyear, 1991; Sorenson & Hales, 2002; Wade et al., 2007). Data suggest that social workers pray with their clients more frequently than clinical psychologists (Canda & Furman, 1999; Hodge, 2007; Shafranske & Malony, 1990; Wade et al.). In a national survey of social workers ($N = 571$), 28% reported having engaged in prayer with their clients during sessions (Canda & Furman). In a sample of gerontological social workers ($N = 299$), 43% of the respondents reported praying with their clients *sometimes* or *often* (Murdock, as cited in Hodge).

Psychologists, however, reported a much lower frequency of praying with clients. In a survey of clinical psychologists ($N = 409$) from Division 12 of the American Psychological Association, only 7% reported praying with their clients (Shafranske & Malony, 1990). Sixty-eight percent of this same sample stated they believed it was inappropriate for a psychologist to pray with a patient.

Data from a survey of secular accredited British counselors ($N = 31$) revealed that 12% openly prayed with their clients either in the past or present (Gubi, 2004). Of counselors in that sample who work with clergy and ministerial referrals, 46% state they have prayed with clients. In a sample of a variety of different types of United States therapists in secular counseling settings, 5% reported praying with or for a client in their most recent session (Wade et al., 2007).

Continuum of Acceptability

It appears that there is a continuum of opinion regarding the acceptability of prayer in counseling. As can be seen in Figure 10.1, some believe that prayer is never acceptable in counseling. On the other hand, some therapists believe that praying with clients is highly effective. Religious

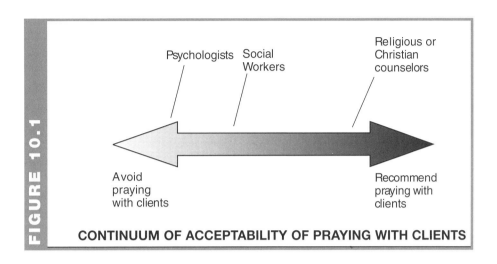

CONTINUUM OF ACCEPTABILITY OF PRAYING WITH CLIENTS

and Christian counselors tend to be on that end of the continuum (Ball & Goodyear, 1991; Sorenson & Hales, 2002; Wade et al., 2007). Therapists who do not believe in God are more likely to be at the other end of the spectrum.

We believe that the overt use of prayer with clients is merited in certain situations. We concur with Weld and Eriksen (2007), who wrote, "Therapists may be remiss in not considering prayer as a possible intervention, because prayer in the proper context may promote client welfare" (p. 130). We also agree with Kelly (1995) who stated,

> My approach is to adopt the position that prayer represents a reasonable, humanly valuable expression of spiritual/religious belief on the grounds that personal spiritual/religiousness, which includes prayer, is generally congruent with good mental health. Moreover, considerable, albeit mixed, research evidence and extensive personal experience support the positive psychosocial and physical benefits of prayer. The practical consequence is that prayer in general may have an appropriate role during counseling and psychotherapy. (p. 226–227)

Reasons to Pray With a Client

Having taken the position stated above, it remains for us to define the parameters in which prayer may be considered a legitimate therapeutic option (Basham & O'Connor, 2005; Kelly, 1995). There are several reasons that a therapist may choose to pray with a client. Praying for our clients is apt to make us feel better about them, change our view of them, and make us more open to insights, regardless of our beliefs in the efficacy of intercessory prayer (McCullogh & Larson, 1999). It has been suggested that prayer with clients increases client trust in the counselor and demonstrates empathy (Koenig & Pritchett, 1998). It may reduce clients' loneliness and build hope in them (Koenig & Pritchett). Frequency of prayer is a demonstrated predictor of well-being (Maltby, Lewis, & Day, 1999). Praying with our clients can increase their ego integration and help them open up to their feelings (Heminski, 1992). It can increase motivation in elderly patients and provide structure for the elderly and families (Abramowitz, 1993; Loewenberg, 1988). Nevertheless, there are those who are less than enthusiastic about counselors praying with their clients (Gubi, 2004; Richards & Bergin, 2005).

Reasons Not to Pray and Ethical Considerations

There are issues and ethical considerations that might dissuade therapists from praying with clients. Laws regarding the separation of church and state may make prayer problematic for those working in government-funded organizations (Genia, 2000; Richards & Bergin, 2005; Richards & Potts, 1995). There may be conflicts within therapists' individual agencies regarding internal policies and procedures (Kelly, 1990, 1995). Psychiatric patients and the severely disturbed are often too unstable to participate in therapeutic prayer. Praying with such clients could break their trust, harm their stability, and make the counselor less objective (Koenig & Pritchett, 1998; Richards & Potts, 1995).

Praying with clients improperly runs the risk of imposing the counselor's values on clients, which violates ethical guidelines (e.g., ACA, 2005) (Gubi, 2004; Kelly, 1990, 1995; Richards & Bergin, 2005; Richards & Potts, 1995; Tan, 1994; Weld & Eriksen, 2007). In addition, therapeutic prayer can be confusing if clients begin to regard the counselor as a spiritual director (Basham & O'Connor, 2005; Frame, 2003; Richards & Bergin; Richards & Potts; Tan). Praying with a client can be a form of self-disclosure and needs to be treated as such (Miller, 2003).

Clients who have unresolved anger or dependency issues with God may transfer these issues onto their counselor (Richards & Bergin, 2005). Research has suggested that differences in ideology between therapists and clients may increase the risk of countertransference (Gartner, Harmatz, Hohmann, Larson, & Gartner, 1990). It is important to ensure that clients do not use prayer as an avoidance technique (Basham & O'Connor, 2005; Gubi, 2004; Kelly, 1990; Tan, 1994). Clients have been known to use their spiritual beliefs and practices as a spiritual bypass to avoid doing genuine psychological work (Cashwell, Bentley, & Yarborough, 2007; Cashwell, Myers, Shurts, 2000). Of course, if the therapist believes that prayer is ineffective, it is better to avoid praying with clients (Kelly, 1990, 1995; Magaletta & Brawer, 1998).

Deciding Whether to Pray

There are several factors to consider when deciding whether to pray with a client. Criteria for consideration include assessment, setting, therapist, client, and referral.

Assessment

It is important to assess clients' religious and spiritual beliefs, practices, and experiences prior to considering praying with a client (Frame, 2003; McCullough & Larson, 1999; Richards & Bergin, 2005; Weld & Eriksen, 2007). An informal assessment may take the form of conversation during the intake interview or early sessions. A more formal assessment might employ devices such as an inventory or spiritual genogram (see chapter 4 for a more detailed discussion).

Setting

The setting is a key factor in considering whether to pray with a client (Frame, 2003; Richards & Bergin, 2005). Therapists who work in a religious setting may be expected to pray with clients (Richards & Bergin; Weld & Eriksen, 2007). Prayer may also be appropriate for private practitioners who counsel religiously devout clients (Richards & Bergin; Weld & Eriksen). This would also be the case for therapists who work with clients in an inpatient setting where religious services are part of the therapy (Richards & Bergin; Weld & Eriksen). Due to conflicts between church and state, however, greater caution should be exercised when working in governmental agencies (Genia, 2000; Richards & Bergin; Richards & Potts, 1995). It is recommended that therapists always consult with their supervisors to ensure that they are in compliance with their agency's policies.

Therapist

The counselor should first examine his or her own motivations when attempting to determine whether it is appropriate to pray with a client. The client's best interests should always be kept in the forefront of such decision making (Miller, 2003; Gubi, 2004). Therapists who have the best results in using prayer with clients have a positive regard for this practice (Canda, 1990) and pray themselves in their personal lives (Magaletta & Brawer, 1998). Positive regard may be defined as believing that prayer will be helpful for clients, that it has the potential to help in their personal development, that it can effect therapeutic change, and that it can advance treatment goals (Canda; Kelly, 1990, 1995; Magaletta & Brawer; Tan, 1994; Weld & Eriksen, 2007). Some suggest that the therapist and client should be of the same religion or at least be spiritually compatible (Basham & O'Connor, 2005; Frame, 2003; Kelly, 1990, 1995; Koenig & Pritchett, 1998; McCullough & Larson, 1999; Richards & Bergin, 2005). Finally, consider prayer if you feel prompted or guided to do so (Richards & Potts, 1995; Weld & Eriksen).

Client

As we have indicated, clients who are severely disturbed are not generally good candidates for therapeutic prayer (Genia, 2000; Richards & Bergin, 2005). Clients who request or initiate prayer, on the other hand, are most likely to respond well to such an approach (Basham &

O'Connor, 2005; Frame, 2003; Gubi, 2004; McCullough & Larson, 1999). At a minimum, clients should show openness to praying during the session (Gubi; Kelly, 1990; Koenig & Pritchett, 1998; Weld & Eriksen, 2007). A simple method to assess for such openness is to determine whether prayer is an existing coping mechanism used by the client (Koenig & Pritchett; Weld & Eriksen). Client–therapist boundaries should be should be sound and be well maintained (Koenig & Pritchett; McCullough & Larson; Weld & Eriksen). Therapists should avoid creating dependency with clients through shared prayer (Gubi, 2001).

Referral

Therapists who are uncomfortable praying with their clients can refer them to a clergyperson or pastoral counselor if they think it would be beneficial (Basham & O'Connor, 2005; Koenig & Pritchett, 1998). They may also consider praying for clients privately and encouraging clients to pray for themselves (Richards & Bergin, 2005). In general, it is a good idea to seek supervision or consultation when praying with clients (Gubi, 2007).

How to Pray With a Client

One may use a passive approach or an active approach when praying with a client (Kelly, 1995; Frame, 2003; Magaletta & Brawer, 1998; McCullough & Larson, 1999; Richards & Bergin, 2005; Weld & Eriksen, 2007). The passive approach relies on the client to initiate prayer (Basham & O'Connor, 2005; Gubi, 2004). This approach is favored if the therapist knows little about prayer, feels uncomfortable about using prayer, is in a new therapeutic relationship, or has a low level of intimacy with the client (Magaletta & Brawer; Weld & Eriksen).

The active approach to praying allows the therapist to initiate prayer (Kelly, 1995; Frame, 2003; Magaletta & Brawer, 1998; McCullough & Larson, 1999; Richards & Bergin, 2005; Weld & Eriksen, 2007). When praying, it is best to keep the prayer short, general, and positive (Koenig & Pritchett, 1998). Consider whether or not it is best to pray on a regular basis with the client (Koenig & Pritchett).

Always be certain to request clients' permission to pray (Richards & Potts, 1995; Weld & Eriksen) and to pray in a manner that is consistent with their beliefs (Canda, 1990; Gubi, 2004; Kelly, 1990; Richards & Bergin; Richards & Potts).

After praying with clients, process their experiences with them at a later time (Basham & O'Connor, 2005; Gubi, 2004; Koenig & Pritchett, 1998; Weld & Eriksen, 2007). Therapists may wish to discuss the potential for transference with clients (Gubi, 2001). Prayer should always be used in conjunction with, and not as a substitute for, proper psychotherapy (Frame, 2003; Richards & Bergin, 2005; Basham & O'Connor). Consider assigning prayer as homework or as a supplement to treatment (Frame; Weld & Eriksen). Finally, if you are praying with a client, be sure to discuss this in supervision to ensure that you are maintaining proper ethical practice (Gubi, 2007).

Effectiveness of Prayer

The status of the research on the effectiveness of prayer is controversial (Cha, 2004; Flamm, 2005). Several researchers have analyzed the effects of intercessory prayer, with mixed results. Some studies have found statistical significance (e.g., Cha & Wirth, 2001; Leibovici, 2001) while others have not (e.g., Benson et al., 2006; Seskevich, Crater, Lane, & Krucoff, 2004). The research design methodologies of studies that have suggested statistically significant findings for intercessory prayer have frequently been drawn into question (see Flamm, 2005; Thornett, 2002).

In an effort to draw conclusions from the research on intercessory prayer, Hodge (2007) performed a meta-analytical review of such studies. He found 17 studies that met his criteria. These studies used a double-blind randomized control methodology. Of the 17 trials, seven resulted in a statistically significant improvement of the intercessory prayer group over the control group(s), while ten did not. After combining the 17 studies for the meta-analysis, results revealed statistical significance for the intercessory prayer group, although the omnibus effect size was small (Hodge).

Vignette

The therapist performed a spiritual and religious assessment of Shawnell so that he could be informed about her beliefs and spiritual development. Because the therapist works in a private practice setting, issues regarding the separation of church and state are not relevant. He knows that Shawnell is a Pentecostal and that she prays several times a day as a coping mechanism. His mother is a Pentecostal, so he is familiar and comfortable with many of the beliefs and customs of that denomination. He has introspected regarding whether his inclination to pray with Shawnell is motivated by his own need and has decided that prayer with Shawnell is likely to have a positive effect on the therapeutic relationship. He also knows that Shawnell is emotionally stable and has good boundaries. In the dialogue that follows, the therapist chooses to ask Shawnell if she would like the two of them to pray together. He could have waited for her to initiate or request prayer, but in this case he felt confident that it would be therapeutically sound to ask if Shawnell would like to pray.

Therapist: Shawnell, do you remember during our first session, you asked me if I was saved?

Shawnell: Of course I do...

Therapist: Although I probably wouldn't classify myself as a born-again Christian, I do consider myself spiritual. And I also believe in the power of prayer ... and have seen research on how effective it is. What would you think about us praying together during the session?

Shawnell: All right, we can try that.

Therapist: Would you like for us to pray for guidance and direction before we get started?

Shawnell: Yes.

Therapist: Would you like to do it or should I?

Shawnell: Go ahead this time. Maybe I'll do it next time.

Therapist: Sure ... [pause] .... Dear God,... we know that you are present with us now, just as you are present wherever we go and whatever we do. Shawnell and I know that you care about every hair on our heads … and we know that you care deeply about every concern or issue that Shawnell has. We ask that your Presence and Spirit guide us today as we work together to benefit Shawnell. Help us to work toward her greatest and highest good. We are thankful for your wisdom and guidance in our lives and specifically in this session right now. Amen.

Shawnell: In Jesus's name, Amen. [pause] … Thank you.

Summary

This chapter focused on the strategy of using prayer as a therapeutic intervention. Although the practice is somewhat controversial due to ethical concerns, studies suggest that mental health professionals pray with clients to varying degrees within their respective professions. There are many benefits to praying with clients, including increased openness to the client and increased client trust. The ethical pitfalls include issues of separation of church and state and the potential imposition of values upon the client. When deciding whether to pray with a client, criteria for consideration include assessment, setting, therapist, client, and referral. Research showing the effectiveness of prayer remains controversial.

Discussion Questions

1. Is prayer a part of your personal life?
2. Do you believe that prayer is effective or helpful?
3. What role, if any, do you see for prayer in therapy?
4. In terms of client spirituality, which religious or spiritual belief systems would you feel most comfortable working with? Which would you feel least comfortable working with?
5. What do you see as the most significant ethical complications of praying with a client?

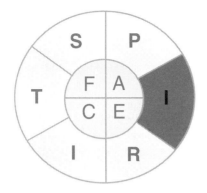

CHAPTER 11

Interpretation
of Sacred Texts

*All scripture is God-breathed and is useful for teaching,
rebuking, and correcting and training in righteousness.*

– 2 Timothy 3:16

Every major religion has some form of sacred text that followers use
as a source of inspiration and guidance (Graham, 1987). There is,
however, tremendous diversity among the different sacred writings, as
well as in their interpretation (Richards & Bergin, 2005). In this chapter, we will discuss interpreting sacred text with clients, the potential
benefits and limitations of this practice, appropriate ethical considerations, and some techniques for enhancing this helping strategy.

Frequency of Reading

People vary in their approach to reading sacred texts. Some may read
their favorite religious texts daily, while others rely on memory, tradition, or the teachings of spiritual leaders (Richards & Bergin, 2005).

The Christian Bible, which is the most widely used sacred text in the United States, is read at least occasionally by 59% of people surveyed (Gallup, 2000). Thirty-seven percent report reading it daily or weekly. Almost two thirds of Americans believe the Bible answers "all or most of the basic questions of life" (Gallup, 2000, ¶ 2). Of particular interest to counselors, 75% state they are very interested or somewhat interested in deepening their understanding of the Bible (Gallup, 2000).

Frequency of Counselors Interpreting Sacred Texts With Clients

Teaching spiritual concepts and referencing scriptures have been found to be the second and third most common spiritual interventions practiced by Christian counselors (Ball & Goodyear, 1991; Richards & Potts, 1995). Although Ellis (1991) believed religion was a source of pathology, he contended that the Judeo-Christian Bible is safely the greatest self-help book ever written (Ellis, 1993). He added that it has probably helped more people than all therapists combined. When therapists' spiritual beliefs differ greatly from those of their clients, the interpretation of sacred texts is a more appropriate therapeutic strategy than prayer (Rabinowitz, 2000).

Research data suggest that the integration of sacred texts in therapy varies significantly for different helping professions. In a national survey of social workers ($N = 1,197$), 59% reported using or recommending spiritual books or writings to their clients (Canda & Furman, 1999). Sixty-four percent stated that they had assisted clients in reflecting critically about their religious or spiritual beliefs. As with prayer, however, psychologists tended to use sacred texts less in their work—approximately half as much as social workers. In a sample of clinical psychologists ($N = 409$), only 32% reported using or recommending religious or spiritual books in therapy (Shafranske & Malony, 1990). In a sample consisting of various types of secular counselors ($N = 73$), 12% reported quoting or referring to scripture in their *just completed* session (Wade, Worthington, & Vogel, 2007).

Potential Benefits of Using Sacred Texts in Counseling

Although there is a paucity of research demonstrating client benefits from discussing sacred texts in counseling sessions, there are studies suggesting that people who regularly read religious material accrue psychological benefits. In a sample of medical patients with major depression, minor depression, or no depression ($N = 1,424$), results indicated that those who read the Bible or other religious material one or more times per day had significantly less depression (Koenig, 2007). In a study of people suffering from persistent mental illness ($N = 406$), those suffering from frustration, hostility, and interpersonal sensitivity tended to turn toward reading sacred texts more frequently (Tepper, Rogers, Coleman, & Malony, 2001). Increased time devoted to religious practices, including scripture reading, resulted in participants' psychological symptoms decreasing and their Global Assessment of Functioning (GAF) scores increasing (Tepper et al.).

The possible benefits to clients of interpreting sacred texts in therapy include:

- increased intellectual understanding and application of the texts (Richards & Bergin, 2005),
- viewing problems from a new perspective (Richards & Bergin; Sperry & Giblin, 1996),
- normalizing problems (Sperry & Giblin),
- a changed belief system (Richards & Bergin),
- better communication with the divine (Richards & Bergin),
- becoming closer with a higher power or experiencing the divine (Richards & Bergin),
- overcoming a sense of isolation (Sperry & Giblin), and
- being comforted or experiencing enjoyment from reading the texts (Richards & Bergin).

Because religious or spiritual texts can provide useful material for discussion, we will now present strategies for incorporating the interpretation of sacred texts into therapy.

Techniques for Interpreting Sacred Texts in Therapy

As with any explicit intervention in the FACE-SPIRIT model—and perhaps especially so with textual interpretation—it is important to assess the client's spiritual beliefs before implementing the strategy. You might ask your client which sacred documents she or he reads, how frequently, and for how long. We would recommend assessing how literally your client generally interprets such texts (see Box 11.1). You might ask the client if particular books or passages give him or her hope, meaning, and a feeling of safety (Miller, 2003). If your client reads scripture frequently, does he or she do so out of a sense of obligation? Ask if he or she experiences joy, guilt, or ambivalence from such reading (Miller).

Sacred texts may be incorporated into a counseling session in different ways. Some of those strategies include the following:

Quote it—There may be times during the session when passages you may know or have previously referenced might serve as timely and effective interventions (Ball & Goodyear, 1991; Miller, 2003; Richards & Bergin, 2005).

Interpret it—Discussing a client's interpretation of a passage can help him or her discover new and deeper meaning in the writings (Ball & Goodyear; Miller; Richards & Bergin).

Indirectly reference it—Through subtly alluding to a passage or parable, you allow the client to make the connection for himself or herself (Ball & Goodyear; Miller; Richards & Bergin).

Discuss stories from the writings—Exploring stories from scripture allows the client to gain clarity, insight, and meaning (Ball & Goodyear; Miller; Richards & Bergin) and draw parallels to his or her own life. For example, the biblical parable of the prodigal son might be a particularly useful story to discuss with a parent who feels abandoned or angry with a child who has abruptly moved out of the home.

Challenge the client's beliefs—Individuals may interpret sacred writings in ways that are ineffective or destructive (Ball & Goodyear;

BOX 11.1

<u>Literalness of Sacred Text</u>

It is important to understand your client's approach to the interpretation of sacred texts. A 2005 Gallup survey asked participants how literally they interpreted the Bible:

- 34% believe the Bible is the actual word of God and should be taken literally
- 48% believe the Bible is the inspired word of God, which need not always be taken literally
- 15% believe the Bible was written by humans and consists of fables, legends, and history

During client intake, or as you begin to discuss sacred texts, you should enquire about your client's views on the origin and nature of his or her sacred text and about how literally he or she believes it should be interpreted.

Eriksen, Marston, & Korte, 2002; Miller; Richards & Bergin). In such cases, challenging clients' interpretations can be therapeutically helpful, if done accurately and in a nonauthoritarian way. We will provide guidelines for doing this in the next section.

Supplement Cognitive Behavioral Therapy (CBT) with scripture— Rather than using logic alone to question automatic thoughts or irrational beliefs, portions of sacred texts can provide a rationale for modifying dysfunctional thinking (Ball & Goodyear; Garzon, 2005; Tan, 1996, 2007)

Encourage the client to read, study, and memorize texts—There may be sections from sacred writings that are comforting during trying life events (Ball & Goodyear; Miller; Richards & Bergin). Particular motivational passages may encourage a client to achieve counseling goals (Eriksen, Marston, & Korte).

As a third party observer—Discuss the role of sacred texts in the development of individuals and society (Hathaway, 2005). This approach may be particularly helpful for clients without strong religious beliefs.

Use sacred texts as an encyclopedia to teach about life—Useful lessons can be gleaned from spiritual or religious documents to teach clients about daily living (Hathaway).

Ask Socratic questions—By asking your client probing and open-ended questions, you may help him or her further deepen and challenge his or her own belief system.

Use a narrative approach—Encourage your client to reinterpret his or her own life story or issue using sacred narratives or parables (Frame, 2003).

Integrate readings with behavioral interventions—This approach can be particularly helpful when training parents to address child-rearing issues (Walker & Quagliana, 2007).

Limitations and Ethical Considerations

As with most interventions, there are caveats, limitations, and ethical concerns that need to be addressed when interpreting sacred texts in therapy. The therapist's attitude in broaching, presenting, and discussing religious or spiritual texts is paramount. For example, it can be harmful to the therapeutic relationship if you use sacred texts in an authoritarian way (Tan, 1996). Do not debate or argue with your client about his or her interpretation (Richards & Bergin, 2005). Since passages in sacred texts are open to numerous interpretations, be open and flexible (Tan). Scrupulously avoid imposing your beliefs or values when working in this realm (Richards & Bergin). Never cite passages to coerce or manipulate your client's behavior, and take care not to oversimplify complex texts in dealing with issues (Tan).

It is important to understand your own hermeneutical limitations (Miller, 2003). If you feel you are going beyond your own understanding or comfort level in wrestling with a text, by all means refer your client to a clergyperson or spiritual leader. Remember, your role is to be a therapist, not a spiritual guide or religious instructor. Both of these roles would constitute a blurring of professional boundaries (Miller). If the client has dysfunctional religious beliefs that emerge in his or her interpretation, refer him or her to a religious leader for guidance

(Richards & Bergin, 2005). On the other hand, respectfully using Socratic questioning may help the client uncover his or her own ineffective or irrational beliefs (Ball & Goodyear, 1991; Garzon, 2005; Tan, 1996).

Vignette

In a counseling session with Shawnell, her therapist learns that she is feeling confused and frustrated about her marriage. As it turns out, her husband has not worked for the past eight or nine years, which has left Shawnell thinking about divorce. Not only is Shawnell feeling angry with her husband for not working, her religious beliefs are causing her to experience guilt for having thoughts about divorce. In the transcript that follows, the therapist explores Shawnell's concerns regarding these issues:

Therapist: Hi, Shawnell, what would you like to talk about today?

Shawnell: Well, not only am I having to deal with my mother, I'm confused and bothered with what to do about my husband and our marriage.

Therapist: It sounds like you're feeling very conflicted. Tell me about your concerns.

Shawnell: I'm just not sure about the marriage anymore. My husband is a kind man and treats me fairly, but … I've started to have thoughts about divorce. It's just that we are both very religious and we know what the Bible says about marriage … and I made a vow to be with him until death do us part.

Therapist: You feel guilty for thinking about leaving, because it goes against your religious beliefs.

Shawnell: Yes … I know divorce is wrong, but it's so hard to keep giving and giving and to receive nothing in return. I guess I wonder if my needs will ever get met.

Therapist: Well it sounds like you're having a difficult time balancing your needs versus the needs of others while also living up to your religious convictions.

Shawnell: Exactly. My needs and the needs of my children.

Therapist: Let's go back to your husband. Are there any particular things that are bothering you about him?

Shawnell: Well ... he doesn't work much ... or should I say he hasn't in the last several years ... maybe it's been 8 to 10 years since he's actually held a job.

Therapist: You must be extremely frustrated.

Shawnell: That's right! I'm mad as heck!

Therapist: Have you talked to him about it?

Shawnell: Yeah ... he says the meek shall inherit the earth ... and he's right ... it is in the Bible you know.

The therapist immediately assumes that this may be a misinterpretation of the passage, as well as a justification for an irrational belief held by Shawnell and perhaps even her husband. Because the therapist is not a biblical scholar, however, he chooses to wait and address the issue in the next session after he has had time to research the meaning of the passage. In the intervening week, the therapist makes a quick call to a religious studies professor at a local university who mentions that the dynamic figure of Moses is paradoxically also considered to be among the meekest of biblical characters. The therapist does some reading using Bible commentaries and the Internet and discovers some surprising material regarding the biblical meaning of meekness. The therapist shares the fruit of his research when he and Shawnell meet again:

Therapist: Shawnell, I'd like to revisit the conversation we had last week about the biblical meaning of meekness. I believe the verse you were talking about was from the Sermon on the Mount; Matthew 5:5 "Blessed are the meek, for they shall inherit the earth."

Shawnell: Yes, that sounds right.

Therapist: What does the word "meek" mean to you?

Shawnell: I don't know ... maybe quiet and passive and ... easy going. My husband is very easy going.

Therapist: I did some research after our session last week, and I think you might find some of it to be quite interesting. Do you know who the meekest man on the face of the earth was, according to the Bible?

Shawnell: No, who?

Therapist: Well according to Numbers 12:3, it was Moses.

Shawnell: Really? I didn't know that!

Therapist: It makes you think, doesn't it? Moses was responsible for the leadership of the entire nation of Israel in the wilderness for 40 years. It was he who stood up to the Pharaoh and demanded that he let the children of Israel go. That doesn't sound like what we generally mean by "meek," does it?

Shawnell: Not by a long shot.

Therapist: In fact, Moses was a very disciplined, "take charge" kind of person. According to William Barclay's Commentary, biblical meekness means to have these qualities. He gives the example of Proverbs, 16:32: "He that rules his spirit is better than he who takes a city."

Shawnell: If that's what "meek" means, I wish my husband were meeker!

After examining meekness from this perspective, Shawnell no longer believes her husband is justified in using a pseudoreligious cover of biblical "meekness" to avoid work. With this new understanding, she is able to develop greater clarity regarding the real issues in her marriage.

Summary

The majority of Americans read the Bible and are interested in deepening their biblical understanding, and referencing sacred texts is the second most common spiritual strategy used by therapists. While the majority of social workers use religious readings in therapy, only a minority of psychologists do. However, research suggests that reading religious texts lowers depression and improves mental health. Discussing sacred texts in session may help clients view their problems differently, change their belief systems, feel closer to their Creator, and be happier.

After doing a spiritual assessment, counselors may approach the use of sacred texts via quotation, interpretation, discussion of stories or parables, and the Socratic exploration of clients' beliefs. CBT and narrative or constructivist approaches are also viable. It is essential to keep your limitations as a subject-matter expert in view at all times and to be cognizant of ethical concerns and the appropriateness of your tone and motivation. Never be argumentative or impose your values or beliefs on clients.

Discussion Questions

1. In the vignette, the therapist used the technique of consulting a religious studies professor in interpreting a sacred text. What are other strategies that could have been used with this client?
2. In a similar scenario with a Muslim client who is citing the Qur'an, would you feel comfortable addressing the text? How might you go about doing so?
3. With which major religions would you feel most comfortable discussing sacred texts (e.g., Hinduism, Buddhism, Islam, Confucianism, Christianity, and Judaism)? What resources could you acquire to enhance your competence?
4. Have you ever addressed religious or spiritual writings during a counseling session? What strategies did you use? What was the result?

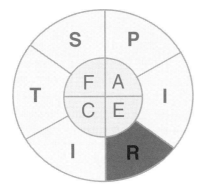

CHAPTER 12

Ritual
Therapy

*It seemed to be a necessary ritual that he should
prepare himself for sleep by meditating under the
solemnity of the night sky ... a mysterious transaction
between the infinity of the soul and the infinity of the universe.*

– Victor Hugo

In this chapter, will discuss the *R* in *SPIRIT,* which represents *Ritual
Therapy.* We will explore how to facilitate and enhance clients' healing and movement toward wholeness through the symbolism inherent
in rituals.

The Therapeutic Aspects of Ritual

Mircea Eliade (1959), the foremost authority on myth and ritual in our
time, alluded to the therapeutic power of ritual in observing that ritual
creates "sacred space" and "sacred time." Similarly, psychotherapists
Imber-Black and Roberts (1992) emphasized that rituals create "protected space" (p. 3). For example, the elements that make up a child's
preparation for bedtime—storytelling, being tucked into bed with a

beloved stuffed animal, or repeating special "good-night" phrases—constitute a ritual that creates security and therapeutically nurtures the child's inner world.

Even simple rituals can be highly effective in fostering wellness, as suggested by research on marital success (Berg-Cross, Daniels, & Carr, 1992). Questionnaires were given to a sample of women married ten years or more, women married three years or less, women divorced ten years or more, and women divorced three years or less. Results indicated that high ritual activity was "associated with long-term marital success" and that "long-term marriages that end in divorce are characterized by significantly less ritual activity than long-term intact marriages" (p. 26). Examples of the kinds of rituals measured by the questionnaires included: talking together in bed before sleeping, using special or pet names with each other, preparing meals together, having special ways of hugging or touching, and attending seasonal religious services together.

"True" rituals are therefore more than repetitive behavior patterns. They may be considered to be *logocentric*, or meaning-creating. Such rituals have the qualities of being validating, integrative, symbolically rich, and curative (Comstock, 1972). They are essential aids in performing the tasks of changing, healing, believing, and celebrating.

The Scope of Ritual Activity

Many types of rituals exist (Imber-Black & Roberts, 1992). *Protorituals*, such as shaking hands, consist of simple actions or verbal interchanges that occur repetitively and more or less spontaneously. More complex *daily rituals* include leaving and returning rituals, bedtime rituals, mealtime rituals, and weekend rituals. To these could be added: lovemaking rituals, fighting and reconciliation rituals, and vacation or holiday rituals. Traditional *cultural rituals* include secular and nonsecular celebrations such as baptisms, bar and bat mitzvahs, pledging allegiance to the flag, and calendar holidays. More intricate are *life cycle rituals,* such as christenings, birthdays, marriages, anniversaries, and funerals. Most complex are the *spontaneous rituals* that are created consciously or unconsciously to deal with personal crises or to mark major life transitions. Rituals can help us negotiate changes connected with divorce, adoption, pregnancy, menopause, recovery from illness, healing from betrayal, recovery from dependency, and even the advent of death. Such rituals may be evolved intuitively; adapted from ceremonies from other cultures; or developed from therapy, meditation, dreamwork, or journaling (Feinstein & Mayo, 1990).

A Typology of Ritual Activity

Many rituals involve practices characteristic of wisdom traditions and can be highly efficacious in assisting clients heal or achieve goals. After surveying a number of wisdom traditions, Parker and Horton (1996) concluded that rituals fall into three general categories, which they labeled as: (1) *celebration or commemoration rituals,* (2) *liberation rituals*, and (3) *transformation rituals*. Therapists can use the three types of rituals to help their clients relate, heal, and change.

Celebration or Commemoration Rituals

Celebration and commemoration rituals honor what has been achieved, express love and caring, affirm relationships, and create a heightened sense of community. Celebration rituals occur frequently, and most individuals have experienced many celebration rituals in their lives. Examples of celebration rituals include throwing a party to honor an achievement such as a promotion, or giving a chip in AA for an anniversary of sobriety.

Commemorative observances are the types of events that are most readily identified as "rituals." These include religious worship services, as well as festivities associated with anniversaries, birthdays, and cultural holidays. Commemoration rituals can be distinguished from transformation rituals (which will be discussed later) in that the former are often cyclic. An anniversary is a commemorative ritual, while a wedding is a transformation ritual. The latter is about getting married. It solemnizes the conversion from singleness to a life of commonality.

The former is about staying married. It celebrates the "story" of the union that came into being as a consequence of marriage.

Commemoration rituals are innately like religious observances in that they are "worship" rituals. The word "worship," however, should be understood in its original meaning of appreciating the "worth-ship" of something. In commemoration rituals, something valuable is honored through remembrance or celebration. The deeper celebratory dimensions of commemorative ritual can be understood by observing the nature of *mythic time*. Eliade (1959) defined mythic time as "reversible" time (p. 68). In mythic time, the past becomes present as one participates in the reality toward which the ritual symbolism points. A traditional theological expression of this dynamic may be found in the Roman Catholic and Eastern Orthodox concept of *anamnesis* (literally, "unforgetting"), which declares that every celebration of the Eucharist not only recalls, but also mystically *participates* in the single, unrepeatable sacrifice of Christ.

The concept of *anamnesis* can also be observed in the common rituals associated with celebrating anniversaries. Married couples often commemorate their anniversary by returning to the restaurant where they courted and ordering the same meals, or by revisiting the place where they honeymooned. They enter a private world by dancing to "their" song. Through these and other means, the couple seeks not merely to remember good times, but to directly reexperience the spark that both began their relationship and keeps it alive. The deepest intent of celebratory rituals is therefore to transcend mere nostalgic reminiscence and achieve *communion*.

Liberation Rituals

While celebratory rituals foster participation in a "sacred past," liberation rituals focus on opening toward the future, promoting catharsis, and providing freedom from painful memories. An example of a liberation ritual might be to write down a persistent negative habit or thought and then burn the paper that it is written on. Liberation rituals are paradoxical in that they may employ an act of destruction to bring forth healing. In liberation rituals, restoration is accomplished via the symbolic removal of, or disengagement from, obstacles to healing. Liberation rituals can help individuals recover from trauma caused by violence, sexual abuse, or betrayal. They enable people to forgive and to reconcile with others by relegating their pain to the past. Negative influences are symbolically terminated, dissipated, or destroyed, and closure is attained. The goal of liberation rituals may therefore be thought of as *release*.

A biblical example of a liberation ritual may be found in the transference of the sins of Israel to the scapegoat on the annual Day of Atonement (Leviticus 16). After the sins of the nation were linked to the sacrificial animal by the high priest through the laying on of hands, the "scape" goat (derived from an Arabic word meaning "remove") was led into the wilderness and released. By this symbolic act, Israel freed herself from her sins by vicariously delivering them into the hands of the demon of the wilderness, Azazel (Graybill, 1987).

Contemporary examples of liberation rituals might include releasing balloons after a funeral to facilitate acceptance of the reality of death. Similarly, one might hold a "string-cutting" ceremony at the time of the finalization of a divorce as a way of turning one's face toward the future and relinquishing unrealistic hopes of reconciliation. Needless to say, for such rituals to be effective, the symbolic activity must be enacted, rather than just thought about. Only as the string is actually cut does the finality of the former spouse's absence register at the level of the unconscious.

A blended family spontaneously evolved a liberation ritual during their weekly trip to the recycling center. Each Saturday, father, son, and stepmother assemble beside the glass recycling bin armed with bags of empty drink bottles. Taking turns, each calls out the name of some exasperating problem or irritation in life, for example, "Mondays!" "homework!" or "car payments!" As the others repeat the name of the problem being "toasted" in unison, the one offering the vexing situation hurls an empty bottle into the metal recycling drum, exorcising the annoyance with a satisfying explosion of broken glass.

While this simple ritual is frequently humorous, it is sometimes solemn and profound. The participants are not afraid to name more weighty adversities, such as the terminal illness of a loved one, or school bullies. So while the ritual has helped the family learn to laugh at their troubles—and they always return from their road trip in a better mood—it also has helped them learn to express empathy and solidarity toward one another. The father and stepmother particularly appreciate the fact that this liberation ritual allows their son to voice concerns that a preadolescent might find very difficult to articulate otherwise (Parker & Horton, 1995).

Transformation Rituals

Finally, transformation rituals signify endings and beginnings and mark entry into new developmental phases. They not only open toward the future and allow closure to occur like liberation rituals, they move us into a "new present" by effecting change. Transformation rituals are rituals of *formation* or *rites of passage*. Through them, something *new* is given birth, affirmed, blessed, or empowered. Eliade (1958) described rites of passage as rituals designed to produce a decisive alteration in the religious or social status of the person being initiated. Traditionally, it is through such rites of passage that boys became men and girls became women. Such rituals typically serve as the doorway to kinship, marriage, authority, tribal membership, and transcendence. Transformation rituals not only announce that changes are occurring; they also facilitate their occurrence. Research suggests, for example, that in societies which have public rituals to mark a young person's coming of age, adolescence is much less problematic than in cultures in which there is no universal agreement about when adulthood is reached (Lefrancois, 1986; Elkind, 1984).

A traditional Sioux transformation ritual is *Hunkapi,* the "making of relatives," associated in the modern imagination with "blood-brotherhood." The two persons who wish to become joined must first perform a sacrificial act to demonstrate the seriousness of their intention. They may cut themselves, fast, or give away some prized possession. Then they symbolically establish their unity by mixing their blood or by being bound together with a cord. As a result, a permanent new sibling relationship is created that will nourish and sustain both partners throughout life (McGaa, 1990).

A modern wife and husband from a religiously mixed marriage created a personal transformation ritual that helped them to declare and to solidify their matrimonial unity. The husband had a Christian upbringing and his wife was Hindu. Both took their religious traditions seriously and were aware that their partner did likewise. Apprehension concerning the potential complications that might arise from such a mixing of traditions created ongoing anxiety for both spouses, particularly for the husband.

During their first year together, the wife, an artisan, crafted a set of beads from rose quartz as a birthday present for her husband. The strand contained 108 beads, the traditional number for a Hindu rosary, or *mala*. However, the wife also attached a small cross to the center bead. When the husband received this gift he was deeply touched by the symbol of religious harmony that his wife had created. He was even more moved when she showed him that she had made an identical rosary for herself, complete with a cross. As the husband and wife ceremoniously placed the beads around each other's neck, they attained a new level of trust and commitment. Through that ritual act, one they pledged to repeat every day, they declared in a new, transformative way their devotion to each other and their willingness to respect each other's faith (Parker & Horton, 1995).

Creating Therapeutic Rituals

According to Parker and Horton (1995), ritual actions and implements can take many forms. Customary ritual actions include storytelling, eulogizing or remembering, eating and drinking, singing or chanting, gift giving, dancing, ritualized touch, game playing, delivering blessings or benedictions, ritual enactments of symbolic creation or destruction, travel or pilgrimage, and prayer or meditation.

Ritual implements come in endless variety, ranging from the *phur-pa,* or Tibetan ritual dagger, to the conventional birthday cake. In planning a ritual, one may choose to imitate the high liturgies of the wisdom traditions by including ritual implements representing some or all of the five senses (Sargent, 1994). Sight may be represented by statues, pictures, candles, icons, memorabilia, or any symbols that are meaningful to the individual. Hearing may be represented by a toast, special music, a benediction or some other form of spoken blessing, bells, drums, or even applause. Taste is commonly represented by sacramental food (such as the aforementioned birthday cake). Smell may be represented by incense, perfume, or flowers. Touch may be represented by holding a feather (Native American), hand-holding, laying on hands or other ritual gestures, dancing, or the use of anointing oil.

In planning rituals, one must consider how to create a protected or sacred space in which the ritual can occur. This may consist of a ceremonial circle, a specially decorated room, an altar, or a more mundane demarcation of sacred space, such as a breakfast table. Closely conjoined with ritual space is ritual time. The boundaries of ritual time may be connected to a sacred calendar, an anniversary, the cycle of the seasons, or—in the case of transition rituals—any significant need or event.

One effective way to practice demarcating and inhabiting sacred space is by creating "altars." Although this might seem to be a dauntingly mystical suggestion, in reality, most people spontaneously create altars in their homes and workplaces. A family picture or photograph of a favorite vacation spot sitting next to the office computer is a functional altar that inspires contemplation and provides comfort. Individuals can consciously choose to create or adorn such simple alters and by doing so exercise their mythic imagination and enlarge their capacity for wonder.

We encourage helping professionals to assist their clients in designing rituals for celebration, liberation, and transformation. The rituals may be done either in the helper's office or in any location that clients choose. It is not necessary for the therapist to be present at the ritual, although in some cases clients may request the helper's participation. We often ask clients to plan a ritual as a homework assignment that will be discussed in the subsequent session.

Vignette

In the next transcript, the therapist helps Dale develop a transformation ritual. Dale was struggling to make sense of his life after inheriting tremendous wealth. Since he no longer had to work to bring in money, Dale was uncertain of what he had to offer to the world. Because he considered himself to be a spiritual person at heart and also to be very sensitive and caring, Dale decided to go back to graduate school and study social work so that he could help others and give back something to society. Through service to others, he hoped to attain a sense of peace and feel less guilty about being so privileged.

Although Dale had reached a tentative career decision, he still felt somewhat insecure about moving from his former field of accounting to a profession that was quite different. Dale had never felt totally congruent as an accountant, however, he still thought of himself as one. For that reason, the therapist believed it might be beneficial to help Dale design a transformation ritual to redefine himself. Through the ritual, Dale might craft a new identity and move more freely into this new phase of his life. The transcript that follows describes Dale and the therapist discussing the ritual.

Therapist: Dale, as I've listened to your concerns about moving into a new field, it occurred to me that you might find it helpful to develop a ritual that would allow you get closure on that part of your life and move into the next.

Dale: You mean like a retirement party? They had a big party for me when I left the firm.

Therapist: Well, parties like that can be a form of celebration ritual, but I'm thinking about a transformation ritual that you could design that would be personally meaningful to you. You would plan it to symbolize your new way of being in the world. If you wished, you and Steve could work on it together, and it could involve as many or as few people as you desired. It could even be done alone, if you wished.

Dale: I like that idea, and I think I would like to include Steve. Since we talked about the flower and how I shut people out, I've been trying to let Steve in more, and I know he would be very supportive. But how do we go about developing a ritual?

Therapist: Well, rituals involve doing something that can serve as a symbolic representation of the issue with which you are concerned. In your case, it sounds like you will want to do something that will give you closure on your old life and mark passage into your new one. You can incorporate important places, food, pictures, music, movements, and any number of other props in your ritual. You can use anything that would be personally significant and symbolic to you. There are no limits, so you can be as creative as you want!

Dale: Wow... this is exciting! I can't wait to start planning it with Steve!

Next Session

Therapist: Hi, Dale. How are you?

Dale: Great!

Therapist: Yes, you do seem very exuberant today!

Dale: Yes, I am! We've planned a ritual that's going to be amazing!

Therapist: Please, tell me more!

Dale: Well, Steve and I are going to take a trip back to the place where our life together began. We're going to have the ritual there in a little park that's just outside the firm where we met. That place has a lot of significance for me because it's where I had my first "real" job, and of course it's where I met Steve. Some of our dearest friends still live in that area, so we've invited them to be a part of our ritual. We haven't seen them in a long time, so having them there will make it even more special.

I'm creating a slideshow that I can play on my laptop that will include lots of pictures of us from back then, music we used to listen to, and pictures of my office and the old apartment building where we lived. Then I'll trace my development from then until now, showing all the places I've lived and worked up to the present. The show will conclude with a section entitled "the future Dale" which will have some pictures of me at the social work agency where I've just started volunteering, and where I hope to eventually work.

We'll have a picnic with food from what used to be our favorite restaurant, and everyone will receive a small, personally-designed appreciation gift from "the real Dale" of today who isn't afraid to let people in.

Then finally, we'll conclude with a symbolic "jumping off" into the future. There's a fountain in the park with a shallow pond and I'm going to jump in it to represent my risking doing something totally new. Of course, knowing my friends, they'll probably all jump off too, but that's okay, maybe they need to make some changes in their own lives!

Therapist: Dale, you seem very excited and confident that this ritual will have a positive impact on your development. Kudos to you for working so hard to make it meaningful, and I look forward to hearing how it goes.

Dale: I am! Thanks so much for suggesting the idea!

The ritual went extremely well for Dale. Steve and his friends were very supportive, and doing the ritual helped Dale to feel more solid in his newly chosen path. Ironically, many of his friends told Dale that they had never really thought his heart was in accounting (even though he was good at it), and they were surprised he hadn't made the change years ago. Having the support of his friends enabled Dale to feel even more confident that he was on the right track.

Because it can sometimes be difficult to make spiritual progress in isolation from others, the therapist also suggested to Dale that he might seek out kindred spirits with whom he could develop a sense of religious community. Dale had once visited a local spiritual community where he felt very much at home and decided to start participating in their activities. By enacting the transformation ritual and making contact with a supportive spiritual community, Dale began successfully moving into his new life role.

Summary

Rituals have been shown to be highly efficacious in healing and can be used for celebration, liberation, and transformation. To be effective, rituals must employ some type of symbolic action, such as touch, speech, or dance. Therapeutic rituals may also incorporate elements that involve all of the senses—including food, scents, pictures, sounds, music, and special locations—to enhance the symbolism that they represent. Helping professionals may assist clients in designing, planning, and sometimes participating in rituals to elicit healing.

Discussion Questions and Activities

1. What type of therapeutic ritual—celebration, liberation, or transformation—might be appropriate for dealing with the following situations?

   a. a blended family resulting from a remarriage
   b. a wounded veteran returning from combat
   c. a child who is afraid of the dark
   d. a college student who is away from home for the first time
   e. a survivor of domestic abuse who has lived independently for one year

2. Design a ritual that could be used in each of the above cases.
3. What are some examples of rituals that you have in your everyday life that are especially meaningful to you? Why?
4. What rituals would you like to incorporate into your life that you do not presently have? How might you develop these?
5. Can you think of other rituals that might be especially effective in healing? Describe the elements that might be included to enhance their therapeutic efficacy.

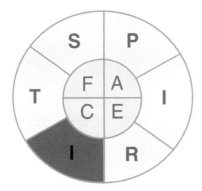

Imagery

Every thing possible to be believed is an image of truth.

– William Blake

Having its roots in antiquity, *imagery,* represented by the second *"I"* in *SPIRIT*, has been used extensively in world religions. In Catholicism, St. Ignatius prescribed meditations that emphasized the use of the visual imagination, Tantric Buddhism relies heavily on visualization practices, and Eastern Orthodoxy has a rich history of using icons as aids to spiritual development. Believing the mind to be a potent healer, many wisdom traditions have utilized the imagination as a means of restoring health and well-being to mind, body, and spirit.

Why Imagery Works

Why does imagery work? Imagery and visualization are closely linked to creativity or "thinking outside the box." Albert Einstein (as cited in

West, 1997) explained how his greatest ideas initially came to him not in words, but in images. By playing with these images, he originated his theories:

> The words or the language ... do not seem to play any role in my mechanism of thought. The psychical entities which seem to serve as elements in thought are certain signs and more or less clear images which can be "voluntarily" reproduced and combined .... This combinatory play seems to be the essential feature in productive thought—before there is any connection with logical construction in words or other kinds of signs which can be communicated to others. (p. 26)

A clue to the efficacy of imagery may be found in brain research. As discussed in chapter 9, while the left hemisphere of the brain is responsible for logic and conscious thought, the right hemisphere governs feelings and the unconscious. According to West (1997), imagery operates on the right hemisphere of the brain and entails nonverbal thinking and consciousness:

> One of the important developments that arose from research on the function of the two hemispheres is the idea that the right hemisphere is thinking at all, that is, the clear demonstration that consciousness and thought are, indeed, possible without words .... How is it that we have so little awareness of this other half of ourselves? One answer is that many functions of the right hemisphere are so fundamental that they are easily taken for granted. Another answer is that the overt concerns of modern culture appear to be almost entirely dominated by the modes of thought most compatible with the left hemisphere, that our view of the world, our educational system, our system of rewards, our aspirations, and our value systems are all effectively focused on reinforcing the operation of the left hemisphere (while the more basic contributions of the right are largely ignored or seen as primitive). (p. 14)

Guided Imagery

Guided imagery, a method of intentionally employing imagery in healing, has been defined as "directed, deliberate, and purposeful elicitation of positive sensory images in an individual's imagination" (Naparstek as cited in Holmes, Mathews, Dalgleish, & Mackintosh, 2006, pp. 54–55). Interestingly, the imagery experience can be so concrete that the bodily senses respond as though the event were actually happening (Epstein, 1986), and numerous studies have shown that imagining doing something is almost as effective as actually doing it.

Extensive empirical research confirms the value of guided imagery in training, rehabilitation, and psychotherapy. For example, guided imagery has been found to have a greater impact on anxiety than verbal processing of the same material and to result in greater increases in positive mood than verbal training (Holmes et al., 2006). Six months after knee surgery, patients who participated in a guided imagery group had significantly greater knee strength and significantly less reinjury anxiety and pain than those in placebo and control groups (Cupal & Brewer, 2001). When compared to a control group, nausea, vomiting, and anxiety were significantly reduced in chemotherapy patients who received guided imagery and relaxation training (Burish, Carey, & Krozley, 1987). Guided imagery was found to be even more effective than relaxation training for breast cancer patients. Guided imagery groups of such patients experienced significantly less depression, anxiety, and fatigue than those in relaxation groups (Goodwin, Lee, Puig, & Sherrard, 2005). Furthermore, in healthy adults, guided imagery and music were found to significantly decrease cortisol levels and depression, fatigue, and mood disturbances, suggesting that this intervention could be of great benefit in combating the physiological effects of stress (McKinney, Antoni, & Kumar, 1997). We believe that imagery also can often be quite effective in helping clients achieve spiritual insight in counseling.

Imagery for Spiritual Insight

Imagery can be incorporated into therapeutic practice in various ways. One method is to invite the client to participate in a guided imagery exercise by closing his or her eyes, taking several deep breaths, relaxing, and imagining that he or she is in a very peaceful place. If the helping professional knows the client well, the description of the place can be tailored to be a setting in which the client would feel most comfortable, such as in a deep forest or by the ocean. If the client's preferences are not known, the described imagery can be left open ended and just described as a place of great peace. The client can then be asked to visualize a very spiritual figure who approaches and has a special message to convey or spiritual gift to give. The spiritual figure might be an angel, a religious figure, a prophet, or even a sacred animal.

Another way to use spiritual imagery is to assign clients homework in which they visualize themselves developing the positive qualities of figures from their own religious traditions. For example, a Hindu might practice visualizing the cultivation of the faithfulness of Hanuman, while a Christian or Jew might visualize the development of the obedience of Abraham or the patience of Job.

Vignette

In the following transcript, we will show how imagery was used with Dale. At this point in his therapy, Dale had begun taking social work classes and was enjoying them and receiving positive feedback on his skills. Almost all of his classmates were women, however, and he was experiencing some self-doubt about going into what appeared to him to be a primarily female profession. Although Dale was gay, he took pride in not being effeminate, and going into a profession dominated by women seemed somehow to threaten his masculinity. Although he was still committed to becoming a social worker, he wanted some reassurance that he wasn't making a mistake.

Therapist: So you've started your social work program. How is that going?

Dale: Even though I know I'm doing the right thing by studying social work, I just really wish I felt more confident and didn't have these nagging self-doubts. I know you won't tell me what to do, but I sure wish somebody would!

Therapist:	I understand that you would really like some reassurance that you're on the right path. Although it's not my role to give that type of advice, you might be able to find those answers by going within. Would you like to try some imagery to see if you can receive any guidance?
Dale:	Sure, I'm willing to try anything to get answers.
Therapist:	All right, Dale. I invite you to close your eyes, get very comfortable, and take several deep breaths. As you breathe in, visualize yourself breathing in peace and deep relaxation, and as you breathe out, imagine all the stress going out with each breath.

Now imagine yourself in a very quiet, peaceful forest. The shade is cool and pleasant, and a gentle breeze is gently caressing your skin. You're enjoying the rich aroma of the earth and of life itself. The birds are chirping softly in the branches above you, and you're delighting in the beautiful colors of the deep green leaves and the bright blue water of a gurgling brook that's flowing along the rocks. As you sit beside the water, you feel very calm and in harmony with your surroundings.

In the distance, you hear a soft rustling and see a figure emerge slowly from a grove of trees. You sense that this figure has something especially for you, which is yours to claim, if you choose. If you wish, you may ask to receive the special gift and it will be given. If you decide to accept the gift, it will be yours to keep and you may use it any way you want. If you desire, you may even accept the gift so completely that it will become a part of you. You will then say goodbye to the giver of the gift, and with a heart full of gratitude, you will feel completely at peace.

When you're ready, you may open your eyes and return to this room.

Therapist:	I notice that you're smiling.
Dale:	Yes, I got my answer. I saw my grandfather, who died many years ago, but who was a big influence on me when I was growing up. He handed me a book that had a picture

on the cover of a man standing valiantly on a small boat on a stormy sea. The man was alone, but in the clouds above him, there were hands that seemed to be blessing him and protecting him from all harm. They were pointing the way home. I have a clear sense that the man in the boat was me and that the Spirit is always there guiding me, if only I remember to look up and listen.

Therapist: How do you feel about your decision to go into social work now?

Dale: I feel totally assured.

We have found that imagery can be very empowering for clients, and that images often leave a more potent and lasting impression than verbal communication ever could. As in Dale's case, the use of imagery can be quite instrumental in helping clients gain insight and achieve peace. Perhaps the old adage is correct: A picture really *is* worth a thousand words. Certainly, in order to facilitate healing, it may be.

Summary

Imagery involves using the imagination to restore health and wholeness to body, mind, and soul. The therapeutic technique of guided imagery consists of inviting the client to relax and visualize a peaceful setting in which he or she is given a special message or gift. The guided imagery experience is then processed with the client to help him or her derive meaning and strength from the insights gained. An alternative method of employing imagery is to assign homework in which clients are asked to visualize how characters from their own wisdom traditions might address their problems, thereby receiving guidance and strength from these images.

Discussion Questions and Activities

1. Play an instrumental piece of music, close your eyes, and let your mind float. What images arise as you listen? What feelings emerge?

2. Describe a scene that you would find personally relaxing. What sights, sounds, smells, tastes, and tactile experiences would be present?
3. How might you help clients replace distressing, negative images with more positive ones? Can you describe some specific examples?
4. Visualize yourself developing the qualities of an inspiring character from your own wisdom tradition or within your own culture. How does it feel to form this picture in your mind?
5. Describe an image that has stayed with you for a long time. What might have caused that image to have such a lasting impact? How has it affected you?

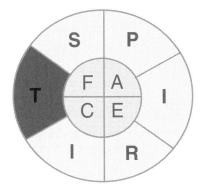

Transgression Relief

Forgiveness, then, is all that need be taught,
because it is all that need be learned.

– Foundation for Inner Peace

People frequently come to counseling because of hurts and wounds from others (Wade, Bailey, & Shaffer, 2005; Wade & Worthington, 2005). However, unless the underlying pain or causative factors are addressed, the resultant dysfunctional behaviors and psychic pain will generally continue (Murray, 2002). *Transgression relief* is a way to address these residual issues (Murray) so that true healing may ensue.

Rather than simply using the traditional term *forgiveness,* we coined the term *transgression relief* to use in the FACE-SPIRIT model for several reasons. First, people tend to have misconceptions regarding what "forgiveness" entails (Enright, 2001; Enright & Fitzgibbons, 2000; Luskin, n.d.; Reed & Enright, 2006). Second, forgiveness has religious connotations, which may be objectionable to some (Rye, 2005). Finally, by placing the emphasis on *relief,* we are attempting to reframe the concept in a decidedly positive way by highlighting the psychological benefits that accrue to the person who has been wronged, rather than focusing on the work that must be done in extending mercy to the wrongdoer. Throughout this chapter, however, we use the terms forgiveness and transgression relief interchangeably.

Forgiveness is an emerging therapeutic approach that is gaining popularity among counselors (Baskin & Enright, 2004). In a sample of secular counselors ($N = 73$), 9% reported discussing forgiveness in their *just completed* session (Wade, Worthington, & Vogel, 2007). Christian counselors have rated forgiveness as the fifth most common spiritual intervention they use (Ball & Goodyear, 1991).

Therapists consider transgression relief to be an important therapeutic intervention (Denton & Martin, 1998; Konstam et al., 2000). In a sample of mental health counselors ($N = 381$), 94% believed it was appropriate for a therapist to bring up forgiveness (Konstam et al.). Over one half (51%) of the participants thought that therapists had the *responsibility* to bring up forgiveness in appropriate situations. In a study of marital and family therapists ($N = 128$), the therapists' openness to client religiosity and the therapists' age explained a large percentage (26%) of the variance in the application of forgiveness therapeutic techniques (DiBlasio & Proctor, 1993).

Data has suggested that most clients want to discuss forgiveness explicitly, although some feel very differently (Wade, Bailey, & Shaffer, 2005). Processing transgression relief can be complex and problematic, especially for groups such as abused women (Lamb, 2002). Research results have revealed two important factors for therapists to consider before engaging in transgression relief (Wade et al.). First, it is important to consider the length of therapy and the level of trust that has been built with clients. Clients are more open to discussing forgiveness if they believe there are an adequate number of sessions available and if they feel safe with their therapist. Second, clients are more willing to engage in forgiveness work if they have adequate ego-strength or self-esteem. If clients are suffering from low ego-strength, it may be necessary to work on improving their self-esteem before engaging in transgression relief (Wade et al.).

There is little consensus in the literature regarding a definition of forgiveness (Denton & Martin, 1998; Macaskill, 2005). However, a review of the definitions for forgiveness reveals a consensus that forgiveness is a positive coping strategy that helps clients reorient their thoughts, feelings, and behaviors toward offenders (Wade & Worthington, 2005). In addition, forgiveness reduces negative emotions such as anger, resentment, and bitterness and fosters positive emotions such as compassion, sympathy, and pity.

Religious and Secular Transgression Relief

Forgiveness is frequently associated with religion, especially in predominately Christian cultures (Denton & Martin, 1998; Wade & Worthington, 2005). The majority of world religions encourage and value transgression relief (Rye, 2005), however, transgression relief can be facilitated with or without any reference to religion (Enright & Fitzgibbons, 2000; Richards & Bergin, 2005).

Studies examining forgiveness facilitated by religious and secular interventions have yielded differing results (Rye, 2005; Rye & Pargament, 2002; Rye, Pargament, Pan, Yingling, Shogren, & Ito, 2005). In one study, researchers treated some groups with a secular forgiveness strategy and the other groups with a parallel religious version (Rye & Pargament). No differences were found between the two groups at posttreatment measurement. In a similar study involving divorced clients, both the secular and religious groups demonstrated significant increases in forgiveness of ex-spouses and in understanding of forgiveness compared to the control group (Rye et al., 2005). The secular group, however, showed greater improvement in the reduction of depressive symptoms. On the other hand, religious forgiveness strategies helped participants feel renewed in their spiritual faith (Rye).

Potential Benefits of Transgression Relief

The success of forgiveness therapy, or transgression relief, has demonstrated a causal relationship between forgiving an injustice and the amelioration of psychological distress (Reed & Enright, 2006).

Research has shown it to be effective in both individual and group therapy settings (Rye, 2005). In a meta-analysis comparing process-based forgiveness treatments in individual and group settings, researchers found that although both were effective, the individual treatment group had a larger effect size on emotional health (Baskin & Enright, 2004). The average effect size in these studies for psychological health using group forgiveness treatment ($N = 3$) was .59 and for individual forgiveness treatment was 1.42 ($N = 2$) (Baskin & Enright). Although the effect size for individual treatment was over twice that of group, we would not discourage group work since its effect size is considered large (Cohen, 1988).

Transgression relief is effective in healing deep emotional wounds, debilitating feelings, and severe trauma, such as incest (Diblasio & Benda, 1993; Lin, Mack, Enright, Krahn, & Baskin, 2004; Reed & Enright, 2006). In a sample of emotionally abused women ($N = 20$) split into a forgiveness treatment group and an alternative treatment group, those in the forgiveness group had statistically less depression, anxiety, and posttraumatic stress symptoms compared to the alternative treatment group, along with an improvement in self-esteem (Reed & Enright). The effect size for this sample was 1.44 (Baskin & Enright, 2004). In a study of female incest survivors ($N = 12$), the treatment group showed statistical improvement in anxiety, depression, forgiveness, and hope compared to the wait-list control group (Freedman & Enright, 1996). When the control group received their intervention, they showed the same pattern of change.

Healing from negative romantic relationships can be aided through forgiveness work (Rye et al., 2005). In study of divorced participants ($N = 149$) being treated in eight-week forgiveness groups, researchers split respondents into three groups: a secular forgiveness group, a religious forgiveness group, and a no-intervention control group (Rye et al.). Both forgiveness groups demonstrated significant improvement in forgiveness of their spouses over the control group.

In a study of an inpatient substance abuse clinic, participants ($N = 14$) were split into two groups (Lin et al., 2004). One group received 12 weeks of forgiveness therapy while the other half received an equal amount of an alternative treatment. Those in the forgiveness group had statistically significant improvements in their trait anger, trait anxiety, depression, self-esteem, and vulnerability to drug use compared to the alternative treatment (Lin et al.).

Researchers have suggested that transgression relief can assist in personality development (Enright, 1994). Data have demonstrated that forgiveness has assisted participants in restoring their faith in God (Enright; Rye & Pargament, 2002). It is also worth noting that in a study of social loneliness, forgiving oneself has been shown to be more important than forgiving others (Day & Maltby, 2005).

Preparing the Client for Transgression Relief

Before you begin transgression relief with your clients, you will want to be sure that they are properly prepared. Attempting to engage clients in the process of forgiveness before they are ready can be ineffective and may possibly create emotional harm (Enright & Fitzgibbons, 2000). Before beginning transgression relief, do the following:

- Acknowledge your clients' suffering, which may include shock and denial.
- Help your clients understand how they have been wronged.
- Validate your clients' sense of injustice.
- Allow clients the opportunity to express feelings of hurt, anger, and resentment.
- Ensure that your clients are safe and that proper boundaries are effectively in place (Enright, 2001; Enright & Fitzgibbons).

Some clients may insist that they have forgiven a wrongdoer out of a sense of wanting to live up to their religious ideals (Frame, 2003; Kanz, 2000). However, your clinical judgment may lead you to suspect otherwise. Pseudoforgiveness can result in depression and anxiety (Kanz). Help the client pursue authenticity by reframing forgiveness as a process (Richards & Bergin, 2005). Acknowledge the work that he or she has done in moving toward forgiveness, but show the client that since transgression relief is a process there may be more work to complete.

Clarifying Misconceptions

It is important to clarify for your clients the common misconceptions that can inhibit the forgiveness process (Luskin, n.d.). First, it is essential that both therapist and client understand the distinction between transgression relief and reconciliation (Enright & Fitzgibbons, 2000; Freedman, 1998; Reed & Enright, 2006; Wade & Worthington, 2005). Forgiveness involves the hurt person giving up his or her resentment toward the wrongdoer. Reconciliation, on the other hand, entails resuming a relationship with the wrongdoer. Forgiveness requires only the hurt person taking action, while reconciliation requires the cooperation of both the perpetrator and the hurt individual (Freedman). The danger of misconception in this area can be illustrated by a study showing that in a sample of the general population ($N = 159$) and Roman Catholic clergy ($N = 209$), both perceived reconciliation as a necessary condition to forgiveness (Macaskill, 2005).

We have found that clients frequently resist forgiveness if they believe that it will require making amends with the wrongdoers. It can be helpful for your clients to understand that they have four choices regarding their decision to forgive and/or reconcile (Freedman, 1998). As seen in Figure 14.1, clients may choose to forgive and reconcile (quadrant I), forgive but not reconcile (quadrant II), not forgive and

	Reconcile	Not Reconcile
Forgive	I forgive and reconcile	II forgive but not reconcile
Not Forgive	III not forgive and reconcile	IV not forgive and not reconcile

FIGURE 14.1

CLIENTS' OPTIONS OF FORGIVENESS AND RECONCILIATION

reconcile (quadrant III), or not forgive and not reconcile (quadrant IV). Clients need this flexibility when doing transgression relief. For example, you may have clients who need to reconcile (e.g., because they work with the wrongdoer) but are not ready to forgive (quadrant III). Alternatively, we find clients who are willing to explore transgression relief only if it involves not meeting or reconciling with the offender. Helping your clients understand these distinctions will allow them to make better decisions and feel more comfortable going forward with the process.

Misconceptions frequently occur regarding transgression relief and concepts such as condoning the behavior, pardoning the wrongdoer, forgetting the offense, and receiving an apology from the wrongdoer (Enright, 2001; Enright & Fitzgibbons, 2000; Luskin, n.d.; Reed & Enright, 2006). Help your clients understand that if they forgive wrongdoers, they are not condoning, pardoning, or forgetting the offense. Help your clients understand that forgiveness is done within oneself; hence, it does not require an apology from the perpetrator.

The Steps in the Forgiveness Process

Counselors have admitted a lack of understanding regarding the steps required for transgression relief (Konstam et al., 2000). There are, however, two primary models in the literature which can assist therapists in this process (Rye, 2005; Wade & Worthington, 2005): the Enright model (Enright & Fitzgibbons, 2000) and the Worthington model (Worthington, 1998). We will examine these models below.

The Enright Model

The Enright model (Enright, 2001; Enright & Fitzgibbons, 2000) consists of 20 steps or processes that occur during four phases:

- Uncovering
- Decision
- Work
- Deepening

In Appendix 14.1, you can see the 20 steps or processes and the four phases of the model. As you can observe from the uncovering phase, the steps begin by examining clients' defenses and anger. Assist them in gaining awareness of the costs of their existing coping strategies, including shame, depleted energy, obsessional thinking, comparing self to the wrongdoer, and the possible additional effects of having a worldview that is colored by bitterness.

In the second phase of the model (decision), therapists assist clients in realizing that their previous coping strategies have been ineffective (Enright & Fitzgibbons, 2000). This insight should encourage a commitment to change. In the third phase (work), therapists help clients reframe their attitudes and develop empathy toward offenders using questions that put them in touch with the humanity of the wrongdoer. Additional steps in this phase focus on helping clients bear the pain of the offense and offering the gift of forgiveness to the wrongdoer.

The final phase of the Enright model (deepening) consists of a series of processes to deepen the forgiveness experience (Enright & Fitzgibbons, 2000). Some of these steps may happen spontaneously during early phases of the treatment. The steps include helping clients: find meaning in suffering, realize that they have needed forgiveness themselves in the past, gain insight into universality, find new purpose in life, and notice changes within themselves.

A strength of the Enright model is that it provides structure for the therapist. We highly recommend that you read chapter five of *Helping Clients Forgive* by Enright and Fitzgibbons (2000), as it further outlines each of the 20 processes.

The Worthington Model

Another useful heuristic is the Worthington (1998) model (note that several of the steps are similar to the Enright model). The Worthington Model (Wade & Worthington, 2005; Worthington) is sometimes referred to as the REACH model:

Recall the hurt or offense
Empathy for the offender
Altruistic gift of forgiveness

Commit to the forgiveness process
Holding on to forgiveness

In the first step of the model, therapists maintain a nonjudgmental and supportive attitude while helping clients Recall the offense (Wade & Worthington; Worthington). This is similar to Enright's uncovering phase.

The second step of the Worthington model (Wade & Worthington, 2005; Worthington, 1998) involves helping clients build Empathy for the wrongdoer by having them imagine the thoughts and feelings of the offender at the time of the event. This step is comparable to steps 12 and 13 of Enright's work phase. Step three is giving the Altruistic gift of forgiveness to the wrongdoer. An element of this process includes helping clients remember times when they were forgiven for their errors. This is similar to step 15 of the work phase in the Enright model.

Next, clients make a public Commitment to forgive the wrong-doer (Wade & Worthington, 2005; Worthington, 1998). The commitment can be either oral or written, and it should be shared with another. Although the Enright model suggests making a commitment to the forgiveness process in the decision phase, it does not encourage clients to share this with another.

The last stage in the Worthington model involves clients Holding onto forgiveness. Having clients reread their written commitment can provide a method for solidifying the positive effects of therapy in the future.

Vignette

During previous counseling sessions, the therapist learned that Shawnell had been harboring resentment and bitterness toward her father for many years. Shawnell's father abandoned the family when Shawnell was a young girl, which was devastating for her. She was unable to forgive him, which made her distrustful of men and affected her current relationship with her husband.

The therapist decides to begin with steps one and two of the Enright model, which involve exploring the client's defenses and anger issues. This is analogous to the Worthington model's first step, which is **R**ecall the hurt. When the therapist inquires into Shawnell's experience, she discusses the pain, sadness, and anger she still feels toward her father for his actions. This provides two benefits. First, it creates a cathartic release for Shawnell while building therapeutic trust as the therapist listens empathically and nonjudgmentally. Second, it highlights how her existing coping strategies are no longer helping her. This will be important during phase two of the Enright model (decision).

Therapist:	Shawnell, you had mentioned previously that you have never forgiven your father for abandoning you and your family when you were five years old. Do you think that is something you might be willing to explore today … forgiving him?
Shawnell:	Sure. It's just something I've had a hard time forgiving him for.
Therapist:	What expectation did you have for him? What should he have done?
Shawnell:	Hmmm. He should have stayed with my mother and our family. He should have supported us financially. That was his responsibility! His duty!
Therapist:	So did he do that?
Shawnell:	No.
Therapist:	What did he do?
Shawnell:	He left us. Never communicated with us … never supported us.
Therapist:	So where was it written that he *must* stay with the family? I realize that it would have been preferable, but where did it say he *must* do that?
Shawnell:	Nowhere.
Therapist:	So Shawnell, what does believing that he should have stayed and supported his family cause you?
Shawnell:	A lot of pain. (Silence) Hurt. It makes me sad and angry.
Therapist:	Is it possible your dad was just doing the best that he could?
Shawnell:	Yes … I guess he really was.

Therapist:	Are you ready to forgive him today? To let him live his life believing he did the best that he could.
Shawnell:	Yes … I think I am. I'm tired of being upset with him.
Therapist:	Good. Let me hear you say, "I forgive him."
Shawnell:	I forgive him!
Therapist:	I'm also going to ask you to pray with your church group, as you had mentioned … that God will help you forgive him. Would that be okay?
Shawnell:	Sure. That sounds good.
Therapist:	One last thing. You had mentioned that your father makes you feel sad and angry. Wasn't there someone else you mentioned that makes you feel sad and angry?
Shawnell:	Oh, my gosh. My husband. I feel the same way about my husband.
Therapist:	And why is that?
Shawnell:	I feel abandoned by him the same way I did by my father … not physically but financially. (Long pause) Did I marry my father?

These valuable insights will prove to be important for Shawnell in addressing her ongoing resentment toward her husband. In the next session, the therapist can pick up phase three of the Enright model (work) and assist Shawnell as she works on transgression relief toward both of the men in her life.

Summary

The term *transgression relief* provides a useful alternative to the more traditional *forgiveness,* because it is free from the misconceptions and religious connotations of forgiveness, and it shifts the focus from the wrongdoer to the self. Transgression relief is a positive coping strategy that helps clients reorient their thoughts, feelings, and behavior toward offenders, which promotes long-term healing. Forgiveness therapies, therefore, have been gaining popularity. There are minor differences between secular forgiveness and religious forgiveness in terms of effectiveness. Research studies suggest transgression relief can be a powerful healing mechanism for both individual and group therapies. Analyses reveal that transgression relief is helpful for healing deep emotional wounds, debilitating feelings, failed romantic relationships, and in recovery from trauma, incest, and substance abuse.

Methods for preparing clients for forgiveness work include listening empathically and clarifying misconceptions about forgiveness. Enright and Worthington provide two models for implementing transgression relief.

Discussion Questions

1. Of the two forgiveness models presented in this chapter, which do you prefer? Why?
2. Are there people in your life that you have not forgiven? What has been the impact on you? What should you do about it?
3. In your opinion, what are the greatest risks of pursuing transgression relief in a therapeutic context?
4. Have you ever done forgiveness work with clients in the past? If so, what happened?

APPENDIX 14.1

THE PHASES AND PROCESS STEPS IN THE ENRIGHT FORGIVENESS MODEL

Uncovering Phase

1. Examination of psychological defenses and the issues involved
2. Confrontation of anger: the point is to release, not harbor, the anger
3. Admittance of shame, when this is appropriate
4. Awareness of depleted emotional energy
5. Awareness of cognitive rehearsal of the offense (obsessional thinking)
6. Insight that the injured party may be comparing self with the injurer
7. Realization that one may be permanently and adversely changed by the injury
8. Insight into a possibly altered "just world" view

Decision Phase

9. A change of heart/conversion/new insights that old resolution strategies are not working
10. Willingness to consider forgiveness as an option
11. Commitment to forgive the offender

Work Phase

12. Reframing, through role-taking, who the wrongdoer is by viewing him or her in context
13. Empathy and compassion toward the offender
14. Bearing/accepting the pain
15. Giving a moral gift to the offender

Deepening Phase

16. Finding meaning for self and others in the suffering and in the forgiveness process
17. Realization that one has needed others' forgiveness in the past
18. Insight that one is not alone (universality, support)
19. Realization that one may have a new purpose in life because of the injury
20. Awareness of decreased negative affect and, perhaps, increased positive affect, if this begins to emerge, toward injurer; awareness of internal emotional release

Adapted from *Helping clients forgive: An empirical guide for resolving anger and restoring hope*, by R. D. Enright, & R. P. Fitzgibbons, 2000, Washington, DC: American Psychological Association.

15

Closing Thoughts & Vignettes

Happiness cannot be traveled to, owned, earned, worn or con-sumed. Happiness is the spiritual experience of living every minute with love, grace and gratitude.

– Denis Waitley

Although we have reached the end of the book, we truly believe that this is only a beginning. In our shared journey, we considered the *why*, *when*, and *how* of incorporating spirituality into counseling and helping. In the *FACE-SPIRIT* model, we explored simple strategies for integrating spirituality into practice—both indirectly and directly—and examined the complexities of working with diverse beliefs. We pondered the importance of spirituality in everyday life and also in situations in which spiritual themes are salient as priorities that deserve special consideration in helping.

At the end of this chapter, we have written additional counseling vignettes to help challenge and stretch your ability to implement the FACE-SPIRIT model. We hope that you will take time individually, or in a group, to review and contemplate these situations. The opportunities to practice now will make implementation easier and smoother in real life.

The Shared Journey

While our time together is now coming to a close, the opportunity to integrate spirituality into helping will continue as each client looks to you with eager expectancy, hoping to find answers. In your shared journey, you will encounter the supreme privilege and ultimate responsibility of entering into an *I/Thou* relationship that may serve as the portal for your client's healing. Will you be ready and willing to create the sacred space within yourself that allows for this encounter to occur?

Knowing how difficult it can be in the hectic pace of the workaday world to focus on *being* rather than *doing,* Abraham Maslow (1991) offered practical tips for living a unitive life—that is, one that would lead toward self-actualization. His suggestions indicate how we can enter and dwell in the Being-realm, where I/Thou relationships can flourish. The following are a few of Maslow's tips:

1. Sample new and fresh experiences, and fight the tendency to always remain with the familiar.
2. Meditate, cultivate periods of quiet, and go into a state of intuitive reverie. Regularly allow yourself time away from clocks, worldly demands, duties, and other people.
3. Love and abide by the eternal, intrinsic laws of the Tao toward other individuals and the whole of nature. Be a good citizen of the universe.
4. Embrace your past and your guilt, while forgiving and being compassionate with yourself. Looking back, try to smile at your own childishness from the past as you might smile at your own grandchild now.
5. To cultivate gratitude, do not compare yourself with others who are luckier than you, but instead with those who are less fortunate.
6. Seek beauty everywhere—in art, music, literature, nature—and contemplate people who are virtuous and worthy of respect.
7. Look at a familiar person or situation as if seeing for the very *first* time. Then gaze at the same familiar person or situation as if seeing for the very *last* time.

8. To be more fully present in the moment, spend time with babies and children, puppies, kittens, monkeys, or apes.

9. Contemplate your life as it might appear to a historian a thousand years in the future. Then think about your life as it might appear to someone living in a remote village in a foreign land. Next, consider your life as seen through the eyes of an ant. Finally, imagine that you have only one year left to live.

10. Try to regain your sense of the miraculous, and cultivate a belief in infinite possibility. Never underestimate the power of each individual, and always remember that it takes only one candle to illuminate a cave.

We believe that Maslow's simple suggestions serve as excellent guidelines for reaching beyond ourselves and fostering our spirituality, thereby allowing us to better assist our clients. By engaging in these activities, we gain leverage by which to renew ourselves and prevent the burnout that often arises when we constantly strive to help others.

Throughout this book, we have emphasized the role of the therapist's spirituality in facilitating clients' healing. We hope that you will nurture your own spiritual development and realize that you have the power to be the catalyst for your clients' change.

Reflecting on the transformative power of the spiritual journey, we are reminded of the words of the great poet, T. S. Eliot, who wrote:

We shall not cease from exploration
And the end of all our exploring
Will be to arrive where we started
And know the place for the first time.

In the words of Albert Einstein (1931), "The most beautiful experience we can have is the mysterious—the fundamental emotion which stands at the cradle of true art and true science" (para. 3). We believe that this experience is also the fountain from which vitality, creativity, and healing may spring forth. It is through communion, stillness, and simplicity, and the resultant freedom from "tyranny of the immediate," that we are liberated to experience true change.

May both you and your clients partake of this mystery, and may you find your lives transformed by the beauty and meaning you discover there. Although the journey may seem perilous at times, the voice of silence and hidden wisdom beckons you.

As the Chinese philosopher Lao-Tzu observed, "The journey of a thousand miles begins with a single step." We wish you well on your own spiritual path and hope that each of your steps will be infused with wisdom, beauty, and peace.

Additional Vignettes

For each of the following vignettes, please consider the following questions:

- What spiritual and/or religious issues might impact this case?
- How might you gain greater understanding regarding the relevant issues?
- Using the FACE-SPIRIT model, what strategies might you employ to address these issues? Please be specific and give concrete examples of how you might use the appropriate FACE-SPIRIT strategies.
- Write a sample dialogue between the mental health professional and client (or an inner dialogue within the helper himself or herself), showing how one (or more) of the FACE-SPIRIT strategies might be employed to address the issues presented in this case.

1. **Sachiko**, a 45-year-old Japanese American female who is a Pure Land Buddhist, has been very depressed since the death of her brother several years ago. Due to major job responsibilities at the time, Sachiko was unable to return to Japan for his funeral but has not been able to stop thinking about it. Her husband suggested that she seek counseling because she seems to have lost interest in life.

2. **Sarah**, a 40-year-old lesbian, has been experiencing turmoil in her present relationship because of her inability to openly express

love and tenderness. As a Catholic child, Sarah was sexually assaulted by an older male cousin in front of a crucifix in her parents' home. Sarah, now a practicing pagan, longs for a deeper spiritual connection and greater intimacy with her partner, although she believes she lacks the ability to completely trust anyone.

3. **Caleb,** a 28-year-old African American male, comes to counseling for depression and anxiety. A paraplegic, Caleb grew up in a Baptist household. When Caleb was 11, his father "found Jesus," dropped his career as a semiprofessional ball player, and became a fervent local minister. Disappointed that he had lost his "hero" (i.e., father) to God, Caleb felt propelled to rebel in his adolescence. At 19, Caleb's path of alcohol, drugs, and petty crimes ended in a police chase and car accident that left him paralyzed from the waist down. After serving three years in prison, Caleb has not been able to hold down a job or maintain a relationship. Hence, his financial situation and social isolation exacerbate his depression and anxiety. He continues to hold anger toward God for "stealing" his father from him.

4. **Vivian**, a 35-year-old case worker is trying to manage her extraordinarily large caseload, make ends meet with very low pay, and deal with the stress associated with being a single parent. She finds herself becoming more and more irritated by her clients and dreads seeing some of the more difficult ones. She has begun to describe herself "as a well that has run dry." It is 8:30 Monday morning, and she is sitting in her office, waiting for her first client to arrive, wondering how she can survive another week.

5. **Jennifer**, age 22, is in love with Tom, the leader of her Buddhist meditation group. They have been living together for two years, and Jennifer is now wondering where the relationship is going. Whenever she asks Tom about the possibility of marriage, however, he tells her that she should meditate more and try to overcome desire and attachment, which are the root causes of all suffering. In counseling, Jennifer reveals that she is depressed and states, "I know that I should be more detached and not put pressure on Tom to make a commitment, but I can't stop doing it. I don't know what's wrong with me that makes me cling to that

which is impermanent. Tom tells me that I need to overcome my sloth and torpor because I'm making us both miserable, but I just don't know how. Can you help me?"

6. **James**, age 55, is an evangelical Christian who is experiencing tremendous guilt regarding his elderly disabled mother. James recently had her placed in an assisted care facility because he feared for her safety living alone. She is most unhappy, however, and lets James know that she hates her new living arrangements. James reveals, "I've done a great wrong because my mother should be allowed to move in with us. I felt I had no choice, though, because my wife was completely against it. She said that she could not hold down her own full-time job and take care of my mother too. I realize my mother can be challenging at times, especially when she is delusional, but the Bible says, "Honor thy father and thy mother," and I'm not doing that. Now I feel I've got to choose between my mother and my marriage, and I don't know what to do." James seeks counseling at the request of his wife.

7. **Annette**, age 40, identifies herself as "spiritual but not religious." She is enthusiastic about various forms of "New Age" spirituality and is always reading some new publication from that genre of spiritual literature. She attends a local "New Thought" Interfaith Fellowship intermittently. She has begun seeing a counselor because of growing feelings of loneliness and self-doubt. She divorced fifteen years ago and has not been in a sustainable, serious relationship since, though she desperately seeks one. She is confused because she spends much time visualizing a partner and other life changes, using meditation techniques that she learns from her church and from her reading.

References

Abramowitz. L. (1993). Prayer as therapy among the frail Jewish elderly. *Journal of Gerontological Social Work, 19,* 69–75.

Adksion-Bradley, C., Johnson, D., Sanders, J. L., Duncan, L., & Holcomb-McCoy, C. (2005). Forging a collaborative relationship between the Black church and the counseling profession. *Counseling and Values, 49,* 147–154.

Ai, A. L., Park, C. L., Huang, B., Rodgers, W., & Tice, T. N. (2007). Psychosocial mediation of religious coping styles: A study of short-term psychological distress following cardiac surgery. *Society for Personality and Social Psychology, 33,* 867–882.

American Counseling Association (ACA). (2005). *ACA code of ethics.* Washington DC: Author.

Archer, S. (2005). Forgiveness linked to less back pain. *IDEA Fitness Journal, 2*(10), 84.

Baer, R. A. (2003). Mindfulness training as a clinical intervention: A conceptual and empirical review. *Clinical Psychology: Science and Practice, 10,* 125–143.

Baer, R. A., Smith, G. T., Hopkins, J., Krietemeyer, J., & Toney, L. (2006). Using self-report assessment methods to explore facets of mindfulness. *Assessment, 19,* 27–45.

Baetz, M., Griffin, R., Bowen, R., Koenig, H. G., & Marcoux, E. (2004). The association between spiritual and religious involvement and depressive symptoms in a Canadian population. *The Journal of Nervous and Mental Disease, 192,* 818–822.

Ball, R. A., & Goodyear, R. K. (1991). Self-reported professional practices of Christian psychotherapists. *Journal of Psychology and Christianity, 10,* 144–153.

Banthia, R., Moskowitz, J. D., Acree, M., & Folkman, S. (2007). Socioeconomic differences in the effects of prayer on physical symptoms and quality of life. *Journal of Health Psychology, 12,* 249–260.

Basham, A., & O'Connor, M. (2005). Use of spiritual and religious beliefs in pursuit of clients' goals. In C. S. Cashwell & J. S. Young (Eds.), *Integrating spirituality and religion into counseling: A guide to competent practice.* Alexandria, VA: American Counseling Association.

Baskin, T. W., & Enright, R. D. (2004). Intervention studies on forgiveness: A meta-analysis. *Journal of Counseling & Development, 82,* 79–90.

Belaire, C., & Young, J. S. (2002). Conservative Christians expectations of non-Christian counselors. *Counseling and Values, 46,* 175–187.

Benson, H., Dusek, J. A., Sherwood, J. B., Lam, P., Bethea, C. F., Carpenter, W., et al. (2006). Study of the therapeutic effects of intercessory prayer (STEP) in cardiac bypass patients: A multi-center randomized trial of uncertainty and certainty of receiving intercessory prayer. *American Heart Journal, 151,* 934–942.

Berg-Cross, L., Daniels, C., & Carr, P. (1992). Marital rituals among divorced and married couples. *Journal of Divorce and Remarriage, 18,* 1–30.

Bergin, A. E., & Jensen, J. P. (1990). Religiosity of psychotherapists: A national survey. *Psychotherapy: Theory, Research, Practice, Training, 27,* 3–7.

Bishop, S. R. (2003). What do we really know about mindfulness-based stress reduction? *Psychosomatic Medicine, 64,* 71–84.

Bjorck, J. P., & Thurman, J. W. (2007). Negative life events, patterns of positive and negative religious coping, and psychological functioning. *Journal for the Scientific Study of Religion, 46,* 159–167.

Bowen Reid, T. L., & Smalls, C. (2004). Stress, spirituality and health promoting behaviors among African American college students. *The Western Journal of Black Studies, 28,* 283–291.

Brady, M. J., Peterman, A. H., Fitchett, G., Mo, M., & Cella, D. (1999). A case for including spirituality in quality of life measurement in oncology. *Psycho-Oncology, 8,* 417–428.

Breslin, M. J., & Lewis, C. A. (2008). Theoretical models of the nature of prayer and health: A review. *Mental Health, Religion & Culture, 11,* 9–21.

Briggs, M. K., Apple, K. J., & Aydlett, A. E. (2004). Spirituality and the events of September 11: A preliminary study. *Counseling and Values, 48,* 174–182.

Briggs, M. K., & Rayle, A. D. (2005). Incorporating spirituality into core counseling courses: Ideas for classroom application. *Counseling and Values, 50,* 63–75.

Briggs, M. K., & Shoffner, M. F. (2006). Spiritual wellness and depression: Testing a theoretical model with older adolescents and midlife adults. *Counseling and Values, 51,* 5–20.

Buber, M. (1970). *I and thou* (W. Kaufmann, Trans.). New York: Scribner's.

Burish, T. G., Carey, M. P., & Krozely, M. G. (1987). Conditioned side effects induced by cancer chemotherapy: Prevention through behavioral treatment. *Journal of Consulting and Clinical Psychology, 55*(1), 42–48.

Burke, M. T., Hackney, H., Hudson, P., Miranti, J., Watts, G., & Epp, L. (1999). Spirituality, religion, and the CACREP curriculum standards. *Journal of Counseling & Development, 77,* 251–257.

Canda, E. R. (1990). An holistic approach to prayer for social work practice. *Social Thought, 16,* 3–13.

Canda, E. R., & Furman, L. D. (1999). *Spiritual diversity in social work practice.* New York: Free Press.

Carlson, T. D., Kirkpatrick, D., Hecker, L., & Killmer, M. (2002). Religion, spirituality, and marriage and family therapy: A study of family therapists' beliefs about the appropriateness of addressing religious and spiritual issues in therapy. *The American Journal of Family Therapy, 30,* 157–171.

Cashwell, C. S., Bentley, P. B., & Yarborough, J. P. (2007). The only way is through: The peril of spiritual bypass. *Counseling and Vales, 51,* 139–148.

Cashwell, C. S., Glosoff, H. L., & Hammond, C. (2007). Spiritual bypass: An exploratory investigation. Unpublished manuscript, University of North Carolina at Greensboro and the University of Virginia.

Cashwell, C. S., Myers, J. E., & Shurts, W. M. (2000). Using the developmental counseling and therapy model to work with a client in spiritual bypass: Some preliminary considerations. *Journal of Counseling & Development, 82,* 403–409.

Cashwell, C. S., & Young, J. S. (2005). Integrating spirituality and religion into counseling: An introduction. In C. S. Cashwell & J. S. Young (Eds.), *Integrating spirituality and religion into counseling: A guide to competent practice.* Alexandria, VA: American Counseling Association.

Cha, K. Y. (2004). Clarification: Influence on prayer on IVF-ET. *The Journal of Reproductive Medicine, 49,* 944–945.

Cha, K. Y., & Wirth, D. P. (2001). Does prayer influence the success of in vitro fertilization-embryo transfer? Report of a masked, randomized trial. *The Journal of Reproductive Medicine, 46,* 781–787.

Chandler, C. K., Holden, J. M., & Kolander, C. A. (1992). Counseling for spiritual wellness: Theory and practice. *Journal of Counseling & Development, 71,* 168–175.

Close, H. T. (1984). Metaphor in pastoral care. *Journal of Pastoral Care, 38*(4), 298–305.

Cohen, J. (1977). *Statistical power analysis for the behavioral sciences* (rev. ed.). New York: Academic Press.

Cohen, J. (1988). *Statistical power analysis for the behavioral sciences* (2nd ed.). Hillsdale, NJ: Elrbaum.

Comstock, W. R. (1972). *The study of religion and primitive religions.* New York: Harper and Row.

Constantine, M. G., Myers, L. J., Kindaichi, M., & Moore, J. L., III (2004). Exploring indigenous mental health practices: The role of healers and helpers in promoting well-being in people of color. *Counseling and Values, 48,* 110–125.

Corey, G. (2005). *Theory and practice of counseling and psychotherapy* (7th ed.). Belmont, CA: Brooks/Cole.

Cowgil, C. (1997). *Carl Jung (1875–1961). Biography.* Retrieved on September 23, 2007, from http://www.muskingum.edu/~psych/psycweb/history/jung.htm

Cupal, D. D., & Brewer, B.W. (2001). Effects of relaxation and guided imagery on knee strength, reinjury anxiety, and pain following anterior cruciate ligament reconstruction. *Rehabilitation Psychology, 46*(1), 28–43.

Day, L., & Maltby, J. (2005). Forgiveness and social loneliness. *The Journal of Psychology, 139,* 553–555.

Denton, R. T., & Martin, M. W. (1998). Defining forgiveness: An empirical exploration of process and role. *The American Journal of Family Therapy, 26,* 281–292.

DiBlasio, F. A., & Benda, B. B. (1993). Practitioners, religion and the use of forgiveness in the clinical setting. *Journal of Psychology and Christianity, 10,* 166–172.

DiBlasio, F. A., & Proctor, J. H. (1993). Therapists and the clinical use of forgiveness. *American Journal of Family Therapy, 21,* 175–184.

Einstein, A. (1931). *Living philosophies.* Retrieved on March 4, 2008, from http:// www.wisdomquotes.com/cat_spirituality.html

Eliade, M. (1958). *Rites and symbols of initiation: The mysteries of birth and rebirth.* New York: Harper & Row.

Eliade, M. (1959). *The sacred and the profane.* New York: Harcourt, Brace & World.

Eliot, T. S. (1943). *The four quartets.* Retrieved on March 5, 2008, from http://www. ubri-aco.com/fq.html

Elkind, D. (1984). *All grown up and no place to go: Teenager in crisis.* Reading, MA: Addison-Wesley.

Ellis, A. (1991). The case against religiosity. In C. Bufe (Ed.), *Alcoholics anonymous: Cult or cure?* San Francisco, CA: Sharpe Press.

Ellis, A. (1993). The advantages and disadvantages of self-help therapy materials. *Professional Psychology: Research and Practice, 24,* 335–339.

Ellis, A. & Schoenfeld, E. (1990). Divine intervention and the treatment of chemical dependency. *Journal of Substance Abuse, 2,* 459–468.

Ellison, C. W. (1983). Spiritual well-being: Conceptualization and measurement. *Journal of Psychology and Theology, 11,* 330–340.

Enright, R. D. (1994). Piaget on the moral development of forgiveness: Reciprocity or identity? *Human Development, 37,* 63–80.

Enright, R. D. (2001). *Forgiveness is a choice: A step-by-step process for resolving anger and restoring hope.* Washington, DC: American Psychological Association.

Enright, R. D., & Fitzgibbons, R. P. (2000). *Helping clients forgive: An empirical guide for resolving anger and restring hope.* Washington, D.C.: American Psychological Association.

Epstein, G. (1986). The image in medicine. *Advances in Medicine, 3,* 22–31.

Eriksen, K., Marston, G., & Korte, T. (2002). Working with God: Managing conservative Christian beliefs that may interfere with counseling. *Counseling and Values, 47,* 48–68.

Faiver, C. M., O'Brien, E. M., & McNally, C. J. (1998). "The friendly clergy": Characteristics and referral. *Counseling and Values, 42,* 217–221.

Feinstein, D., & Mayo, P. E. (1990). *Rituals for living and dying: From life's wounds to spiritual awakening.* New York: HarperCollins.

Flamm, B. L. (2005). Prayer and the success of IVF. *The Journal of Reproductive Medicine, 50,* 71.

Foss, L. L., & Warnke, M. A. (2003). Fundamentalist Protestant Christian women: Recognizing cultural and gender influences on domestic violence. *Counseling and Values, 48,* 14–23.

Foundation for Inner Peace. (1976). *A course in miracles.* New York: Penguin Books.

Foundation for Inner Peace. (1992). *Psychotherapy: Purpose, process, and practice. An extension of the principles of a course in miracles.* Mill Valley, CA: Author.

Foundation for Inner Peace. (1996). *A course in miracles.* New York: Penguin Books.

Fowler, J. W. (1981). *Stages of faith: The psychology of human development and the quest for meaning.* San Francisco: Harper.

Frame, M. W. (2003). *Integrating religion and spirituality into counseling: A comprehensive approach.* Pacific Grove, CA: Brooks/Cole–Thompson Learning.

Frankl, V. (1984). *Man's search for meaning.* New York: Simon and Schuster.

Freedman, S. (1998). Forgiveness and reconciliation: The importance of understanding how they differ. *Counseling and Values, 42,* 200–216.

Freedman, S. R., & Enright, R. D. (1996). Forgiveness as an intervention goal with incest survivors. *Journal of Consulting and Clinical Psychology, 64,* 983–992.

Freud, S. (1928). *The future of an illusion.* New York: Liveright.

Gadamer, H. G. (1986). *The relevance of the beautiful and other essays.* Cambridge: Cambridge University Press.

Gallup. (2000). *Six in ten Americans read bible at least occasionally.* Retrieved on March 15, 2008, from http://www.gallup.com/poll/2416/Six-Ten-Americans-Read-Bible-Least-Occasionally.aspx

Gallup. (2005). *U.S. vs. Canada: Different reads on the good book.* Retrieved on March 15, 2008, from http://www.gallup.com/poll/14512/US-vs-Canada-Different-Reads-Good-Book.aspx

Gallup. (2006). *Religion.* Retrieved March 7, 2006 from http://poll.gallup.com/content/default.aspx?ci=1690

Gangaji (1995). *You are that*. Boulder: Satsang Press.

Garrett, J. C. (1994). The prayer of Francis of Assisi: A counselor's prayer. *Counseling and values, 39*, 73–76.

Gartner, J., Harmatz, M., Hohmann, A., Larson, D., & Gartner, A. F. (1990). The effect of client and counselor values on clinical judgment. *Counseling and Values, 35*, 58–62.

Garzon, F. (2005). Interventions that apply scripture in psychotherapy. *Journal of Psychology and Theology, 33*, 113–121.

Geertsma, E. J., & Cummings, A. L. (2004). Midlife transition and women's spirituality groups: A preliminary investigation. *Counseling and Values, 49*, 27–36.

Genia, V. (2000). Religious issues in secularly based psychotherapy. *Counseling and Values, 44*, 213–221.

George, L. K., Ellison, C. G., & Larson, D. B. (2002). Explaining the relationships between religious involvement and health. *Psychological Inquiry, 13*, 190–200.

George, L. K., Larson, D. B., Koenig, H. G., & McCullough, M. E. (2000). Spirituality and health: What we know, what we need to know. *Journal of Social and Clinical Psychology, 19*, 102–116.

Gladding, S. (1989). *Uses of metaphors and poetry* (videorecording). Alexandria, VA: American Counseling Association.

Goodwin, L. K., Lee, S. M., Puig, A. I., & Sherrard, P. A. D. (2005). Guided imagery and relaxation for women with early stage breast cancer. *Journal of Creativity in Mental Health, 1*(2), 53–66.

Graham, W. A. (1987). *The written word: Oral aspects of scripture in the history of religion.* Cambridge, MA: Cambridge University Press.

Graybill, J. B. (1987). Scapegoat. In *The new international dictionary of the Bible*. Grand Rapids, MI: Zondervan.

Griffith, B. A., & Griggs, J. C. (2001). Religious identity status as a model to understand, assess, and interact with client spirituality. *Counseling and Values, 46*, 14–25.

Grosch, R. J. (1988). The use of metaphor in marital counseling. *Currents in Theology and Mission, 15*(3), 258–262.

Gubi, P. M. (2001). An exploration of the use of Christian prayer in mainstream counseling. *British Journal of Guidance & Counseling, 29*, 425–434.

Gubi, P. M. (2004). Surveying the extent of, and attitudes towards, the use of prayer as a spiritual intervention among British mainstream counselors. *British Journal of Guidance & Counseling, 21*, 461–476.

Gubi, P. M. (2007). Exploring the supervision experience of some mainstream counselors who integrate prayer in counseling. *Counseling and Psychotherapy Research, 7*, 114–121.

Hall, T. W., & Edwards, K. J. (2002). The spiritual assessment inventory: A theistic model and measure of assessing spiritual development. *Journal for the Scientific Study of Religion, 41*, 341–357.

Harrison, M. O., Koenig, H. G., Hays, J. C., Eme-Akwari, A. G., & Pargament, K. I. (2001). The epidemiology of religious coping: A review of recent literature. *International Review of Psychiatry, 13*, 86–93.

Hathaway, W. L. (2005). Scripture and psychological science: Integrative challenges & callings. *Journal of Psychology and Theology, 33*, 89–97.

Hayes, S. C., Strosahl, K., & Wilson, K. G. (1999). *Acceptance and commitment therapy: An experiential approach to behavioral change.* New York: Guilford Press.

Hebert, R. S., Dang, Q., & Schulz, R. (2007). Religious beliefs and practices are associated with better mental health in family caregivers of patients with dementia: Findings from the REACH study. *American Journal of Geriatric Psychiatry, 15*, 292–300.

Heminski, K. E. (1992). *Living presence: A Sufi way to mindfulness and the essential self.* New York: Tharcher.

Hillman, J. (1990). The great mother, her son, her hero, and the puer. In *Father and Mothers.* Dallas, TX: Spring.

Hinterkopf, E. (1994). Integrating spiritual experiences in counseling. *Counseling and Values, 38,* 165–175.

Hodge, D. R. (2007). A systematic review of the empirical literature on intercessory prayer. *Research on Social Work Practice, 17,* 174–187.

Holmes, E. A., Mathews, A., Dalgleish, T., & Mackintosh, B. (2006). Positive in interpretation training: Effects of mental imagery versus verbal training on positive mood. *Behavior Therapy, 37*(3), 237.

Horton-Parker, R. J., & Brown, N. W. (2002). *The unfolding life: Counseling across the lifespan.* Westport, CT: Bergin & Garvey.

Hovey, J. D., & Seligman, L. D. (2007). Religious coping, family support, and negative affect in college students. *Psychological Reports, 100,* 787–788.

Imber-Black, E., & Roberts, J. (1992). *Rituals for our times.* New York: HarperCollins.

Ingersoll, R. E. (1994). Spirituality, religion, and counseling: Dimensions and relationships. *Counseling and Values, 38,* 98–111.

Jensen, J. P., & Bergin, A. E. (1988). Mental health values of professional therapists: A national interdisciplinary study. *Professional Psychology: Research and practice, 19,* 290–270.

Johnson, R. A. (1987). *Ecstacy: Understanding the psychology of joy.* San Francisco: HarperCollins.

Jones, R. T., Kephart, C., Langley, A. K., Parker, M. N., Shenoy, U., & Weeks, C. (2001). Cultural and ethnic diversity issues in clinical child psychology. In C. E. Walker and M. C. Roberts (Eds.), *Handbook of clinical child psychology* (3rd ed., pp. 955–973). New York: Wiley.

Jormsri, P., Kunaviktikul, W., Ketefian, S., & Chaowalit, A. (2005). Moral competence in nursing practice. *Nursing Ethics, 12,* 582–594.

Jung, C. (1962). *Modern man in search of soul* (W. S. Dell & C. F. Baynes, Trans.). New York: Harcourt Brace. (Original work published 1933)

Kabat-Zinn, J. (1982). An outpatient program in behavioral medicine for chronic pain patients based on the practice of mindfulness meditation: Theoretical considerations and preliminary results. *General Hospital Psychiatry, 4,* 33–47.

Kabat-Zinn, J. (2003). Mindfulness-based interventions in context: Past, present, and future. *Clinical Psychology: Science and Practice, 10,* 144–156.

Kaczorowski, J. M. (1989). Spiritual well-being and anxiety in adults diagnosed with cancer. *Hospice Journal, 5,* 105–116.

Kanz, J. E. (2000). How do people conceptualize and use forgiveness? The forgiveness attitudes questionnaire. *Counseling and Values, 44,* 174–188.

Kass, J. D., Friedman, R., Leserman, J., Zuttermeister, P. C., & Benson, H. (1991). Health outcomes and a new index of spiritual experience. *Journal of the Scientific Study of Religion, 30,* 203–211.

Kelly, E. W., Jr. (1990). Counselor responsiveness to client religiousness. *Counseling and Values, 35,* 69–72.

Kelly, E. W., Jr. (1994). The role of religion and spirituality in counselor education: A national survey. *Counselor Education and Supervision, 33,* 227–237.

Kelly, E. W., Jr. (1995). *Spirituality and religion in counseling and psychotherapy: Diversity in theory and practice.* Alexandria, VA: American Counseling Association.

King, D. E., & Bushwick, B. (1994). Beliefs and attitudes of hospital inpatients about faith healing and prayer. *Journal of Family Practice, 39,* 349–352.

King, M., Speck, P., & Thomas, A. (1999). The effect of spiritual beliefs on outcome from illness. *Social Science & Medicine, 48,* 1291–1299.

Koenig, H. G. (2006). Religion, spirituality and aging. *Aging & Mental Health, 10*(1), 1–3.

Koenig, H. G. (2007). Religion and depression in older medical inpatients. *American Journal of Geriatric Psychiatry, 15,* 282–291.

Koenig, H. G., McCullough, M., & Larson, D. B. (2001). *Handbook of religion and health: A century of research reviewed.* New York: Oxford University Press.

Koenig, H. G., & Pritchett, J. (1998). Religion and psychotherapy. In H. G. Koenig (Ed.), *Handbook of religion and mental health* (pp. 324–337). San Diego, CA: Academic Press.

Konstam, V., Marx, F., Schurer, J., Harrington, A., Lombardo, N. E., & Deveney, S. (2000). Forgiving: What mental health counselors are telling us. *Journal of Mental Health Counseling, 22,* 253–267.

Kornfield, J. (1993). *A path with heart.* New York: Bantam.

Kornfield, J. (2005). *Kindness meditation practice.* Retrieved June 29, 2005 from http://dharma.ncf.ca/introduction/instructions/metta.html

Krishnamurti, J. (1991). *The collected works of J. Krishnamurti.* Dubuque, IA: Kendall/Hunt.

Kristeller, J., & Johnson, T. J. (2005). Cultivating loving-kindness: A two-stage model for the effects of meditation on compassion, altruism and spirituality. *Zygon: Journal of Religion and Science, 40,* 391–407.

La Roche, A. N., & Frankel, A. (1986). Time perspective and health. *Health Education Research, 1,* 139–142.

Lamb, S. (2002). Women, abuse, and forgiveness: A special case. In S. Lamb & J. G. Murphy (Eds.), *Before forgiving: Cautionary views on forgiveness in psychotherapy* (pp. 151–171). Oxford, England: Oxford University Press.

Landis, B. J. (1996). Uncertainty, spiritual well-being, and psychosocial adjustment to chronic illness. *Issues in Mental Health Nursing, 17,* 217–231.

Lao-Tsu. (2003). *Tao te ching: The definitive edition* (J. Star, Trans.). New York: Penguin/Putnam.

Lao-tzu. (6th c. B.C.). *The way of Lao-tzu.* Retrieved on March 18, 2008 from http://www.quotationspage.com/quote/24004.html

Leary, M. R., Tate, E. B., Allen, A. B., Adams, C. E., & Hancock, J. (2007). Self-compassion and reactions to unpleasant self-relevant events: The implications of treating oneself kindly. *Journal of Personality and Social Psychology*, *92*(5), 887–904.

Lefrancois, G. (1986). *Of children* (5th ed.). Belmont, CA: Wadsworth.

Leibovici, L. (2001). Effects of remote, retroactive intercessory prayer on outcomes in patients with bloodstream infection: Randomized controlled trial. *British Medical Journal, 323,* 1450–1451.

Levinas, I. (1985). *Ethics and infinity*. Pittsburgh, PA: Duquesne University Press.

Lin, W.-F., Mack, D., Enright, R. D., Krahn, D., & Baskin, T. W. (2004). Effects of forgiveness therapy on anger, mood, and vulnerability to substance use among inpatient substance-dependent clients. *Journal of Consulting and Clinical Psychology, 72,* 1114–1121.

Linehan, M. M. (1993a). *Cognitive–behavioral treatment of borderline personality disorder.* New York: Guilford.

Linehan, M. M. (1993b). *Skills training manual for treating borderline personality disorder.* New York: Guilford.

Loewenberg, F. M. (1988). *Religion and social work practice in contemporary American society.* New York: Columbia University Press.

Lukoff, D., Lu, F., & Turner, R. (1992). Toward a more culturally sensitive DSM-IV: Psychoreligious and psychospiritual problems. *The Journal of Nervous and Mental Disease, 180,* 673–682.

Luskin, F. (n.d.). Nine steps to forgiveness. *Forgive for Good.* Retrieved January 23, 2006, from http://www.learningtoforgive.com/steps.htm

Lustyk, M. K. B., Beam, C. R., Miller, A. C., & Olson, K. C. (2006). Relationships among perceived stress, premenstrual symptomatology and spiritual well-being in women. *Journal of Psychology and Theology, 34,* 311–317.

Macaskill, A. (2005). Defining forgiveness: Christian clergy and general population perspectives. *Journal of Personality, 73,* 1237–1265.

Magaletta, P. R., & Brawer, P. A. (1998). Prayer in psychotherapy: A model for its use, ethical considerations, and guidelines for practice. *Journal of Psychology and Theology, 26,* 322–330.

Maltby, J., Lewis, C. A., & Day, L. (1999). Religious orientation and psychological well-being: The role of the frequency of personal prayer. *British Journal of Health Psychology, 4,* 363–378.

Maltby, J., Lewis, C. A., & Day, L. (2008). Prayer and subjective well-being: The application of cognitive-behavioral framework. *Mental Health, Religion & Culture, 11,* 119–129.

Maslow, A. H. (1991). How to experience the unitive life. *Journal of Humanistic Education and Development, 29,* 109–112.

May, R. (1989). *The art of counseling* (rev. ed.). New York: Gardner Press.

McCarthy, B. (Producer), & Ewing, W. (Director). (1990). *A gathering of men* [Film]. Burlington, Vermont: Mystic Fire Videos.

McCullough, M. E., & Larson, D. B. (1999). Prayer. In W. R. Miller (Ed.), *Integrating spirituality into treatment* (pp. 85–110). Washington, DC: American Psychological Association.

McCullough, M. E., & Worthington, E. L. (1994). Models of interpersonal forgiveness and their applications to counseling: Review and critique. *Counseling and Values, 39,* 2–14.

McCullough, M. E., Hoyt, W. T., Larson, D. B., Koenig, H. G., & Thoresen, C. (2000). Religious involvement and mortality: A meta-analytic review. *Health Psychology, 19,* 211–222.

McGaa, E. (1990). *Mother earth spirituality.* San Francisco: Harper.

McKinney, C. H., Antoni, M. H., & Kumar, M. (1997). Effects of guided imagery and music (GIM) therapy on mood and cortisol in healthy adults. *Health Psychology, 16*(4), 390–400.

Mickley, J. R., Soeken, K., & Belcher, A. (1992). Spiritual well-being and hope for among women with breast cancer. *Image-Journal of Nursing Scholarship, 24,* 267–272.

Miller, G. A. (2003). *Incorporating spirituality in counseling and psychotherapy: Theory and technique.* Hoboken, NJ: John Wiley & Sons.

Moore, T. (1992). *The care of the soul.* New York: HarperCollins.

Muhaiyaddeen, M. R. B. (1981). *A book of God's love.* Philadelphia: Fellowship Press.

Murray, R. J. (2002). The therapeutic use of forgiveness in healing intergenerational pain. *Counseling and Values, 46,* 188–198.

Myers, J. E., Sweeney, T. J., & Witmer, J. M. (2000). The wheel of wellness counseling for wellness: A holistic model for treatment planning. *Journal of Counseling & Development, 78,* 251–266.

Myers, J. E., & Truluck, M. (1998). Health beliefs, religious values, and the counseling process: A comparison of counselors and other mental health professionals. *Counseling and Values, 42,* 106–123.

Myers, J. E., & Williard, K. (2003). Integrating spirituality into counselor preparation: A developmental, wellness approach. *Counseling and Values, 47,* 142–155.

Ñanomoli, T. (1987). The practice of loving-kindness (metta) as taught by the Buddha in the Pali Canon. *The Wheel Publication No. 7.* Kandy, Sri Lanka: Buddhist Publication Society.

Neukrug, E. S., & Fawcett, R. C. (2009). *Essentials of testing and assessment: A practical guide for counselors, social workers, and psychologists.* Belmont, CA: Thomson Brooks/Cole.

O'Connor, M. (2004). A course in spiritual dimensions of counseling: Continuing the discussion. *Counseling and Values, 48,* 224–240.

O'Connor, M., Guilfoyle, A., Breen, L., Mukhardt, F., & Fisher, C. (2007). Relationships between quality of life, spiritual well-being, and psychological adjustment styles for people living with leukemia: An exploratory study. *Mental Health, Religion & Culture, 10,* 631–647.

Oord, T. J. (Ed.). (2007). *The many facets of love: Philosophical explorations.* Newcastle, UK: Cambridge Scholars.

Pargament, K. I. (1997). *The psychology of religion and coping.* New York: Guilford.

Pargament, K. I., Koenig, H. G., Tarakeshwar, N., & Hahn, J. (2004). Religious coping methods as predictors of psychological, physical and spiritual outcomes among medically ill elderly patients: A two-year longitudinal study. *Journal of Health Psychology, 9,* 713–730.

Parker, R., & Horton, H. S., Jr. (1995). Blessing ourselves and others: Rituals to enhance well-being and strengthen relationships. *Virginia Counselors Journal, 23,* 50–61.

Parker, R., & Horton, H. S., Jr. (1996). A typology of ritual: Paradigms for healing and empowerment. *Counseling and Values, 40,* 82–97.

Patanjali. (1982). *The yoga sutras of Patanjali* (A. Shearer, Trans.). New York: Bell Tower.

Pate, R. H., Jr., & Hall, M. P. (2005). One approach to a counseling and spirituality course. *Counseling and Values, 49,* 155–160.

Phillips, R. E., III, & Stein, C. H. (2007). God's will, God's punishment, or God's limitations? Religious coping strategies reported by young adults living with serious mental illness. *Journal of Clinical Psychology, 63,* 529–540.

Poloma, M. M., & Pendleton, B. F. (1989). Exploring types of prayer and quality of life: A research note. *Review of Religious Research, 31,* 46–53.

Poloma, M. M., & Pendleton, B. F. (1991). The effects of prayer and prayer experiences on measures of general well-being. *Journal of Psychology and Theology, 19,* 71–83.

Quackenbos, S., Privette, G., & Klentz, B. (1985). Psychotherapy: Sacred or secular? *Journal of Counseling & Development, 63,* 290–293.

Rabinowitz, A. (2000). Psychotherapy with orthodox Jews. In P. S. Richards & A. E. Bergin (Eds.), *Handbook of psychotherapy and religious diversity* (pp. 237–258). Washington DC: American Psychological Association.

Ramon, E. (2005). The matriarchs and the Torah of hesed (loving-kindness). *Nashim: A Journal of Jewish Women's Studies and Gender Issues, 10,* 154–177.

Reed, G. L., & Enright, R. D. (2006). The effects of forgiveness therapy on depression, anxiety, and posttraumatic stress for women after spousal emotional abuse. *Journal of Consulting and Clinical Psychology, 74,* 920–929.

Richards, P. S., & Bergin, A. E. (2005). *A spiritual strategy for counseling and psychotherapy* (2nd ed.). Washington, DC: American Psychological Association.

Richards, P. S., & Potts, R.W. (1995). Using spiritual interventions in psychotherapy: Practices, successes, failures, and ethical concerns of Mormon psychotherapists. *Professional Psychology: Research and Practice, 26,* 163–170.

Richards, T. A., & Folkman, S. (1997). Spiritual aspects of loss at the time of a partner's death from AIDS. *Death Studies, 21,* 527–552.

Rogers, C. R. (1946). Significant aspects of client-centered therapy. *American Psychologist, 1,* 415–422.

Rogers, C. R. (1949). The attitude and orientation of the counselor in client-centered therapy. *Journal of Consulting Psychology, 13*(2), 82–94.

Rogers, C. R. (1957). The necessary and sufficient conditions of therapeutic personality change. *Journal of Consulting Psychology, 21*(2), 95–103.

Rye, M. S. (2005). The religious path toward forgiveness. *Mental Health, Religion & Culture, 8,* 205–215.

Rye, M. S., & Pargament, K. I. (2002). Forgiveness and romantic relationships in college: Can it heal the wounded heart? *Journal of Clinical Psychology, 54,* 419–441.

Rye, M. S., Pargament, K. I., Pan, W., Yingling, D. W., Shogren, K. A., & Ito, M. (2005). Can group interventions facilitate forgiveness of an ex-spouse? A randomized clinical trial. *Journal of Consulting and Clinical Psychology, 73,* 880–892.

Samuelson, M, Carmody, J., Kabat-Zinn, J., & Bratt, M. A. (2007). Mindfulness-based stress reduction in Massachusetts correctional facilities. *The Prison Journal, 87,* 254–268.

Sargent, D. (1994). *Global ritualism.* Minnesota: Llewellyn.

Seaward, B. L. (1995). Reflections on human spirituality for the worksite. *American Journal of Health Promotion, 9,* 165–168.

Segal, Z. V., Williams, J. M. G., & Teasdale, J. D. (2002). *Mindfulness-based cognitive therapy for depression: A new approach to preventing relapse.* New York: Guilford Press.

Selby, J. (2003). *Seven masters, one path: Meditation secrets from the worlds' greatest teachers.* New York: HarperCollins.

Seskevich, J. E., Crater, S. W., Lane, J. D., & Krucoff, M. W. (2004). Beneficial effects of noetic therapies on mood before percutaneous intervention for unstable coronary syndromes. *Nursing Research, 53,* 116–121.

Shafranske, E. P., & Malony, H. N. (1990). Clinical psychologists' religious and spiritual orientations and their practice of psychotherapy. *Psychotherapy, 27,* 72–78.

Sorenson, A. M., Grindstaff, C. F., & Turner, R. J. (1995). Religious involvement among unmarried adolescent mothers: A source of emotional support? *Sociology of Religion, 56,* 71–81.

Sorenson, R. L., & Hales, S. (2002). Comparing evangelical Protestant psychologists trained at secular versus religiously affiliated programs. *Psychotherapy: Theory/Research/ Practice/Training, 39,* 163–170.

Souza, K. (2002). Spirituality and counseling: What do counseling students think about it? *Counseling and Values, 46,* 213–217.

Sperry, L., & Giblin, P. (1996). Marital and family therapy with religious persons. In E. P. Shafranske (Ed.), *Religion and the clinical practice of psychology* (pp. 511–532). Washington DC: American Psychological Association.

Stanard, R. P., Sandhu, D. S., & Painter, L. C. (2000). Assessment of spirituality in counseling. *Journal of Counseling & Development, 78,* 204–210.

Steen, R. L., Engels, D., & Thweatt, W. T., III. (2006). Ethical aspects of spirituality in counseling. *Counseling and Values, 50,* 108–117.

Summit on spirituality: Counselor competencies (May, 1996 rev.). (1997, Spring). *ACES Spectrum, 57,* 16.

Tan, S.-Y. (1994). Ethical considerations in religious psychotherapy: Potential pitfalls and unique resources. *Journal of Psychology and Theology, 22,* 389–394.

Tan, S.-Y. (1996). Religion in clinical practice: Implicit and explicit integration. In E. P. Shafranske (Ed.), *Religion and the clinical practice of psychology* (pp. 365–387). Washington, DC: American Psychological Association.

Tan, S.-Y. (2000). Religion and psychotherapy. In A. E. Kazdin (Ed.), *Encyclopedia of Psychology* (Vol. 7, pp. 42–46). Washington DC: American Psychological Association and Oxford University Press.

Tan, S.-Y. (2007). Use of prayer and scripture in cognitive–behavioral therapy. *Journal of Psychology and Christianity, 26,* 101–111.

Tarakeshwar, N., Vanderwerker, L. C., Paulk, E., Pearce, M. J., Kasl, S. V., & Prigerson, H. G. (2006). Religious coping is associated with the quality of life of patents with advanced cancer. *Journal of Palliative Medicine, 9,* 646–657.

Templeton, J. (1999). *Agape love: A tradition found in eight world religions.* Philadelphia: Templeton Foundation Press.

Tepper, L., Rogers, S. A., Coleman, E. M., & Maloney, H. N. (2001). The prevalence of religious coping among persons with persistent mental illness. *Psychiatric Services, 52,* 660–665.

Thera, N. (1962). *The heart of Buddhist meditation (Satipa·t·thāna): A handbook of mental training based on the Buddha's way of mindfulness, with an anthology of relevant texts translated from the Pali and Sanskrit.* London: Rider.

Thornett, A. M. (2002). Cautious approach is needed. [Comment/reply to Leibovici (2001).] *British Medical Journal, 324,* 1037.

Tillich, P. (1957). *Dynamics of faith.* New York: Harper & Row.

Tolle, E. (1999). *The power of now: A guide to spiritual enlightenment.* Novato, CA: New World Library.

Utsey, S. O., Lee, A., Bolden, M. A., & Lanier, Y. (2005). A confirmatory test of the factor validity of scores on the spiritual well-being scale in a community sample of African Americans. *Journal of Psychology and Theology, 33,* 251–257.

Vacek, E. C. (1994). *Love, human and divine: The heart of Christian ethics.* Washington, DC: Georgetown University Press.

Wade, N. G., Bailey, D. C., & Shaffer, P. (2005). Helping clients heal: Does forgiveness make a difference? *Professional Psychology: Research and Practice, 36,* 634–641.

Wade, N. G., & Worthington, E. L. Jr. (2005). In search of a common core: A content analysis of interventions to promote forgiveness. *Psychotherapy: Theory, Research, Practice, Training, 42,* 160–177.

Wade, N. G., Worthington, E. L., Jr., & Vogel, D. L. (2007). Effectiveness of religiously tailored interventions in Christian therapy. *Psychotherapy Research, 17,* 91–105.

Waitley, D. (2008). Spirituality quotes. Retrieved on March 19, 2008 from http://www.wisdomquotes.com/cat_spirituality.html

Walker, D. F., & Quagliana, H. L. (2007). Integrating scripture with parent training in behavioral interventions. *Journal of Psychology and Christianity, 26,* 122–131.

Wampold, B. E. (2001). *The great psychotherapy debate: Models, methods, and findings.* Mahwah, NJ: Erlbaum.

Weil, S. (1973). *Waiting on God.* London: Collins.

Weld, C., & Eriksen, K. (2007). The ethics of prayer in counseling. *Counseling and Values, 51,* 125–138.

West, T. G. (1997). *In the mind's eye.* New York: Prometheus Books.

Whitman, W. (1860). Song of Myself. Retrieved March 4, 2009 from http://www.daypoems.net/poems/1900.html

Wiggins-Frame, M. (2005). Spirituality and religion: Similarities and differences. In C. S. Cashwell & J. S. Young (Eds.), *Integrating spirituality and religion into counseling: A guide to competent practice.* Alexandria, VA: American Counseling Association.

Williams, L. M. G., Duggan, D. S., Crane, C., & Fennell, M. J. V. (2006). Mindfulness-based cognitive therapy for prevention of recurrence of suicidal behavior. *Journal of Clinical Psychology: In Session, 62,* 201, 210.

Winterowd, C., Harrist, S., Thomason, N., Worth, S., & Carlozzi, B. (2005). The relationship of spiritual beliefs and involvement with the experience of anger and stress in college students. *Journal of College Student Development, 46,* 515–529.

Wong, Y. J., Rew, L, & Slaikeu, K. D. (2006). A systematic review of recent research on adolescent religiosity/spirituality and mental health. *Issues in Mental Health Nursing, 27,* 161–183.

Worthington, E. L., Jr. (1998). The pyramid model of forgiveness: Some interdisciplinary speculations about unforgiveness and the promotion of forgiveness. In E. L. Worthington, Jr. (Ed.), *Dimensions of forgiveness: Psychological research & theological perspectives* (pp. 107–137). Philadelphia, PA: Templeton Foundation Press.

Wubbolding, R. E. (1993). *Reality therapy with children.* Cincinnati, Ohio: Center for Reality Therapy.

Yalom, E. D. (1989). *Love's executioner: & other tales of psychotherapy.* New York: HarperCollins.

Young, J. S., Cashwell, C. S., & Shcherbakova, J. (2000). The moderating relationship of spirituality on negative life events and psychological adjustment. *Counseling and Values, 45,* 49–57.

Index